ESCAPING
THE DARKNESS

ALSO BY
CORNELL BUNTING

Escaping a Life Sentence

Bunt Walk: A Collection of Poems

The Bellman

Children's Books

Lion with No Roar

Nostril Adventures

Peedie Likes the Drip Drops

Download Chapter 1 at:
CornellBunting.com

ESCAPING
THE DARKNESS

USING ADVERSITY
TO FIND PURPOSE

CORNELL BUNTING

O'LEARY
PUBLISHING
The Influencer's Press

NAPLES, FL

Published in the United States by
O'Leary Publishing
www.olearypublishing.com

The views, information, or opinions expressed in this book
are solely those of the authors involved and do not necessarily
represent those of O'Leary Publishing, LLC.

The author has made every effort possible to ensure the accuracy of
the information presented in this book. However, the information
herein is sold without warranty, either expressed or implied.
Neither the author, publisher, nor any dealer or distributor of this
book will be held liable for any damages caused either directly or
indirectly by the instructions or information contained in this book.
You are encouraged to seek professional advice before taking any
action mentioned herein.

ISBN: 978-1-952491-21-4 (print)
ISBN:978-1-952491-22-1 (ebook)
Library of Congress Control Number: 2021909974.

Editing by Heather Davis Desrocher
Proofreading by Juliann Thomason
Cover and interior design by Jessica Angerstein

Printed in the United States of America

This book is dedicated to my boys,
for being my rock when I was facing hard times in jail.
My love for you boys pulls me through.

Indeed, I will make a path
through the mighty waters,
a way through the wilderness,
and rivers in the desert . . .

~ ISAIAH 43:16

CONTENTS

PART I ADVERSITY & PURPOSE

PART II THE LESSONS

PREFACE

Life is about one thing above all else: purpose. For the one who has found his or her purpose, life is beautiful. For the one who is living devoid of purpose, life can be an intolerable hell. When adversity comes to the person without purpose, life seems pointless. When adversity comes to the person with purpose, life takes on special meaning. Purpose reframes adversity.

Adversity comes to us all. Sometimes it comes to us in droplets — one at a time. But at other times, the floodgates open, and adversity surges over us like a rushing river. We fear that we will be consumed, drowned, and swept away by it. Adversity is an equal opportunity destroyer. It does not care if your collar is white or blue. The wise person cannot reason a way around it. The strong one cannot fight a way through it. The rich person cannot buy a way out of it. Adversity will come to everyone in various ways and to different degrees. Your challenge, and mine, is simply to let our purpose guide us through adversity.

The greatest thinkers of our time have taught us to use the power of purpose to overcome the greatest obstacles. Adversity is not strong enough to destroy you unless you surrender to it. You may be lost in the desert or wading through the deep waters. You may be struggling in the wilderness or walking through the fire. But your rivers of pain, loss, and difficulty cannot drown you. The fires of adversity and trauma are not strong enough to consume you if you can discover (or remember) your purpose.

While your purpose may not be clear to you at the moment, you must remember that it was determined long before this current crisis. Your path was being carved for you from before you took your first breath. You may have been living unaware of the divine intervention that leads us to the one great thing that gives our life meaning. Sometimes, adversity is needed to remind us of our purpose. Other times, adversity can be the vehicle that clarifies our purpose. This has been my experience. When everything was taken from me, when I faced heartbreaking adversity and was in darkness, I found my purpose — and adversity ushered in the light that helped me to escape from the dark.

As the lovely Bible verse in Isaiah promises, you will discover a pathway through the wilderness and water in the desert. You will be renewed and refreshed as you see a way through the deep waters. And you will see that the fires of adversity burn up all that does not serve you.

This desert imagery is rich with power and promise. The reference to the desert is made again and again throughout literature. But it is not just the desert that is present in these ancient texts. It is the juxtaposition of the desert and rivers, the desert and the sea, the desert and plentiful waters. This imagery seeks to open our minds to the possibility that even in the most unusual places, amazing things can happen. Even in the desert, we can find places of abundance. Even in the darkness, we can find the light. Even in jail, we can find our purpose. Our job is to have the faith to believe that a path will be made for us.

Do not be dismayed by the brokenness of the world. All things break. And all things can be mended. Not with time, as they say, but with intention. So, go. Love intentionally, extravagantly, unconditionally. The broken world waits in darkness for the light that is you.

~ L.R. KNOST

INTRODUCTION

In the darkest desert and through the wilderness of adversity, I discovered the path meant for me. After months in the darkness of a jail cell, the light of my purpose shone through for me to see. I discovered that I am a storyteller.

When I was on a journey around the world, I found myself talking with elders in South Africa. One of those elders in Soweto told me that I am meant to inspire others, and bring light to the darkness, through the power of stories – my own, as well as those of others. So, before I take you on this journey of escaping the darkness, let me share a story from the land of my ancestors.

Acres of Diamonds
by Earl Nightingale

An African farmer heard tales about other farmers who had made millions by discovering diamond mines. These tales so excited the farmer that he could hardly wait to sell his farm and go prospecting for diamonds himself. He sold his farm and spent the rest of his life wandering the African continent, searching unsuccessfully for the gleaming gems that brought such high prices in the markets of the world. Finally, worn out and in a fit of despondency, he threw himself into a river and drowned.

The man who bought his farm happened to be crossing the small stream on the property one day when suddenly there was a bright flash of blue and red light from the stream bottom. He bent down and picked up a stone. It was a good-sized stone, and admiring it, he brought it home and put it on his fireplace mantel as an interesting curiosity.

Several weeks later a visitor picked up the stone, looked closely at it, hefted it in his hand, and nearly fainted. He asked the farmer if he knew what he'd found. When the farmer said, no, that he thought it was a piece of crystal, the visitor told him he had found one of the largest diamonds ever discovered. The farmer had trouble believing this. He told the man that his creek was full of such stones, not all as large *as the one on the mantel, but sprinkled generously throughout the creek bottom.*

The farm the first farmer had sold so that he might find a diamond mine, turned out to be one of the richest diamond mines on the entire African continent. The first farmer had owned, free and clear... acres of diamonds. But he had sold them for practically nothing, to look for diamonds elsewhere.

The moral is clear: If the first farmer had only taken the time to study and prepare himself to learn what diamonds looked like in their rough state, and to thoroughly explore the property he had before looking elsewhere, all of his wildest dreams would have come true.

The thing about this story that has so profoundly affected millions of people is the idea that each of us is, at this very moment, standing in the middle of our acres of diamonds. If we only had the wisdom and patience to intelligently and effectively explore our corner of the world, and ourselves, we would most likely find the riches we seek — whether they be financial or intangible or both.

As Socrates said, true wisdom is to Know Thyself. When Socrates penned those words over two thousand years ago, it was for a play in which one character utters the iconic line to another, insisting that he should consider his place and purpose in the universe. It's easy to say but tough to do. Yet it is a necessary step if you plan to live your purpose. You have to know who you are. You have to know what you do NOT know and what your limits are.

It may seem nonsensical to suggest that people should know themselves. Doesn't everyone already know themselves? The answer is a resounding NO. Sadly, most people don't know themselves and repeat the same destructive patterns that bring them unhappiness. The paths to peace are lost to them because they have not done the deep introspective work required to know exactly who they are and exactly what they want. But who could blame them? The plunge into our psyches is a scary trip, indeed. As William Butler Yeats said,

IT TAKES MORE COURAGE TO EXAMINE THE DARK CORNERS OF YOUR SOUL THAN IT DOES FOR A SOLDIER TO FIGHT ON A BATTLEFIELD.

Your soul is a scary place. Therein lives all of your hurts, pains, and disappointments. Looking deep within, you may discover the things about you that you dislike the most: your flaws, inconsistencies, fears, lies, and defects. We all have a monster or two living inside of us. But we have to slay those dragons if we expect to find the treasures that lie deep below the surface. As Rainer Maria Rilke said,

OUR DEEPEST FEARS ARE LIKE DRAGONS GUARDING OUR DEEPEST TREASURE.

The good news is that when you embark on the journey to Know Thyself, in addition to all of the things you dislike or fear, you will find all of the great things that make you who you are. Your skills, gifts, and talents are the buried treasure that must be unearthed now to take you to the next level of life.

In the business world, interviewers call these strengths and weaknesses. We've all had to answer that difficult and surprisingly intrusive question when we are asked to list what is great about us and what may present a challenge for a future employer. Few people are comfortable singing their praises, but they have to answer the question if they want to get the job. So, they do.

Similarly, though, we do not want to reveal to a total stranger the elements of our personality that we dislike or hide. Instead, we come up with an answer that is neither truthful nor revealing to make it through the interview. But we know that some places inside of us need to be exposed to the light. While we don't want to expose them in an interview, during our own time of stillness and quiet, we can look at those questions and answer them honestly.

The process of self-discovery is not an easy one. It is the most difficult thing you will experience. This is not about who you are now. I don't care who you are. Nobody does (except maybe your mother). The real question is who and what you are destined to be. One way to start is to answer this question:

WHAT CAN I CREATE IN THE WORLD THAT WOULD NEVER HAVE EXISTED WITHOUT ME?

The answer might be a song, a chair, a book, a game, a hairstyle, a company, a school, an orphanage, a charity, a baked good. The truth is — it doesn't matter. The point is to lay your hand on something that will never come into the world without your involvement.

We live in a culture where people say "love yourself," "take care of yourself," "be yourself." It seems as if we want to love ourselves, but we struggle to find something about ourselves that is truly lovable. We are trapped in cycles of self-deprecation, comparison to others, and chronic complaining. We don't look good enough; we don't weigh the right amount; the rips and muscles aren't in the spots we want them; we aren't married to the right person; our children don't behave as we want; we don't live where we want; we don't live how we want.

Some people live their dreams. Other people spend money to watch people who are living their dreams. It's quite a paradigm shift. Every time we sit down to watch a basketball game, a movie, a television show, or a concert, we are watching someone's blood, sweat, and tears come to fruition. We pay for that all-important look into their lives. But the performance is only a tiny part of it. Sure, celebrities and wealthy people live lavish lives. I'll concede that. They take expensive vacations, wear the finest clothes, and live in the lap of luxury. But they pay a high internal price for the millions of dollars they earn. For some, the price is too high and ends in drug overdose, alcohol poisoning, or suicide. But for others, they are high on life, doing what they love to do, being where they want to be. Nine hours in the studio is not a drudgery for them. It's heaven. Hitting a thousand golf balls for a professional golfer is like a trip to the amusement park.

The real question is, are you living your life or are you watching others live theirs? You need to have a 360-degree view of your life. Here is how I see it:

THE PAST GIVES YOU EXPERIENCE, WISDOM, AND PERSPECTIVE.

THE PRESENT SHOULD BRING YOU PEACE, PURPOSE, AND CONTENTMENT.

THE FUTURE IS MEANT TO PROVIDE HOPE, AMBITION, AND EXCITEMENT.

Together, all three perspectives help you to be the best person you can be with an outlook on life that is always hopeful, content, and expectant. Dreams that don't come to fruition can bring disappointment, but our limited vision for the future can never compete with God's all-knowing perspective. As we yield ourselves to Him, we can be certain that He is still lovingly directing our steps even when we don't see the path ahead. (Proverbs 16:9)

So how did I come to Know Myself? How did I find my purpose? This is the story of how adversity helped me to find my purpose - how I escaped the darkness and found the light - and how you can too.

PART 1

Adversity & Purpose

Owning our story can be hard but not nearly
as difficult as spending our lives running from it.

Only when we are brave enough to explore the darkness
will we discover the infinite power of our light.

— BRENÉ BROWN

Time isn't precious at all, because it is an illusion. What you perceive as precious is not time but the one point that is out of time: The Now. That is precious indeed. The more you are focused on time — past and future — the more you miss the Now, the most precious thing there is.

— ECKHART TOLLE

CHAPTER 1

THE SUN WAS SHINING

2013

I was in a good place. I truly loved my life and had everything a man could want. I was finally happy and the sun was shining. So, I decided that I needed to make some evaluations. And that led to something unexpected, something I was not prepared for and did not know exactly how to handle. I have always given people the benefit of the doubt. And I knew that when I trusted people, I could be setting myself up for an attack. I knew what people were capable of. I had seen the best of humanity as well as the worst. But this time . . . this time I didn't know that I was setting myself up for a fall into a deep, dark hole.

My focus was on making money. This was all-consuming, and it took me into a shadowy world. My life was no longer filled with quality time: family, picnics, trips to the amusement park, and date nights. Suddenly I was living in a whole new, unexpected world. It was something I had to go through and, hopefully, would survive. This was a part of the journey. And I was a journeyman.

I was embroiled in contracts and making big deals. After a while, I was so blinded by the work, I could no longer see my family, even though they were staring me right in the face. I was as good as a blind man. I had lost the present moment. I was fixated on the future and it cost me the ability to appreciate the life I had. The darkness had found me and chained me to the underworld.

> **Someone I loved once gave me a box full of darkness.**
> **It took me years to understand that this, too, was a gift.**
>
> — **MARY OLIVER,** *THIRST*

I was in a new environment now with new clients. And those clients did not trust the people I trusted. They wanted assurances I was unable to give. I tried to make a case to them about why it was feasible to let me choose the team to work on their projects. But they were not assured. I was living under a cloud. Adversity was coming and I was going to be smack dab in the middle of it.

CHAPTER 2

THE STORM

July 2013

It was a rainy Friday afternoon. I was wining and dining with a friend of mine as I drove through the winding roads of the city. Suddenly the cloudless starlit night was broken by flashes of red and green. As I pulled to the side, I could not imagine what I might have done.

"License and registration, please," the officer said, tapping on the glass with the butt end of a flashlight.

"Handle this, man!" one of the passengers said from the rear of the car.

I rolled the window down. "Good evening, officer."

"License and registration!" he repeated.

"What seems to be the problem, sir?"

"Speeding. Don't make me ask again."

I reached for my wallet and handed the documents to the officer.

"Let's go, man," the big boss said. "You aren't going to sit here and wait for him to come back. Are you?"

"Well, I can't go now. He knows who I am, he has my license."

"You bring trouble down on my head, man, I will spread your body across the city like butter. You understand?"

"Just stay calm. It's going to be fine." I spoke the words but I did not believe them.

The officer returned moments later. "This license isn't coming up in my system. What did you do—buy it in an alley?"

I chuckled nervously. "Come on, officer. It's a valid license. Can you run it again?"

"I already ran your plate two miles back. Tell me, is this vehicle stolen."

That wiped the smile off my face. "Stolen? Of course not. Hey man, what is this anyway?"

I knew something bad was about to go down. This wasn't adding up. My thoughts were interrupted by the sound of sirens coming from every direction. The glare of the lights lit up the dark sky. They were ready for something big to happen. I was in shock.

"Stay cool," the big boss said as the vehicle was surrounded by blue uniforms and badges. "Nobody says a word about our business. If you do, I'll kill you. Understand?"

My head was spinning. I barely remembered the door flying open and the strong arm of the officer pulling me from my seat and onto the ground. They lifted me from the ground shouting questions and commands at me from every direction. I couldn't tell who was speaking. There were just mouths moving, fingers pointing, and hands throwing me this way and that way.

I waited to hear the words that would let me know that I was being arrested and was in serious trouble:

You have the right to remain silent. Anything you say can and will be used against you in a court of law. You have the right to an attorney. If you cannot afford an attorney, one will be appointed to you. Do you understand these rights as I have read them?

I would have said yes to the warning if I had heard it. But I never heard it. They were going to take me without reading me my rights. Something was wrong. Very wrong. This was something that was being cooked up. I could tell. This was a plot. My mind ran wild trying to figure out the chaos. But there was no understanding. A master plot had been hatched and I was right in the middle of it. I was being pushed out of a plane with no parachute. So, I had to learn how to fly on the way down or I was going to hit the ground hard.

My mind was running at a hundred miles an hour. I thought about all the different possibilities that could have led to this moment. But none of them played out. Someone had set me up. I hoped it would unfold with my release—mistaken identity, or something. But things were not moving in that direction. This was as serious as it got. So, I decided to close my mouth and refuse to speak. I thought that nothing could be held against me if I stayed silent.

I put my head down and listened to the voices that were still shouting around me. Suddenly, certain words started to rise about the other . . . terrifying words.

"Murder."

"Killing."

"Where is the body?"

> Another secret of the universe: Sometimes pain was like a storm that came out of nowhere. The clearest summer could end in a downpour. Could end in lightning and thunder.
>
> — BENJAMIN ALIRE SÁENZ

I finally realized that this was no ordinary traffic stop or fake charge. They were trying to pin me to a murder. This was as serious as it could be. It made no sense. Now I was sure it had to be a case of mistaken identity. There was no way they could be trying to frame me for a murder. Impossible. But those were the words I heard coming from the pursed lips and clenched teeth of the officers around me.

What would I do?

The next thing I heard were the voices of my passengers and a lot of commotion behind me. The situation was escalating. I tried to plan the next few hours of my life. I was no longer living day by day. I was living minute by minute. I thought through what I would do when they got me to the police station. I was entering a deep pit that could easily swallow me whole. My future was uncertain. I had no frame of reference. I would have to let it unfold. There was no other choice. I would be an observer. It was the best I could do . . . for now.

Prison is a second-by-second
assault on the soul, a day-to-
day degradation of the self,
an oppressive steel and brick
umbrella that transforms seconds
into hours and hours into days

— MUMIA ABU-JAMAL

CHAPTER 3

FREEDOM OR DEATH

August 2013

The cell walls were moving. It felt as if they were rolling and melting all around me. The dim light above me only reminded me of the darkness that surrounded me. One inmate in the corner emanated such putrid smells, I wondered how long it would be before he vomited up the steak dinner he had been enjoying just a couple of hours earlier. The sounds of the jail were threatening. There were loud voices, crashes, and clangs that reminded me that I was a prisoner. The bile rose from my belly and rested on my tongue.

I let my eyes scan the cell and look over the faces of the other inmates there with me. One man was covered in muscles and tattoos. He was staring right back at me. Another looked like he lived in the jail. He wore an old trench jacket and a crumpled hat. I couldn't figure out how he had been allowed to come in with a coat and cap. He reeked of alcohol and kept singing a song about a sailor and the sea. Two boys who didn't look old enough to be in jail were huddled in conversation. There were seven men in all. All men whose lives had taken the same wrong turn as mine had. All who were lost and desperate. How did I get here? How did these other men arrive at this horrific state? What was the answer for me, and all the other men crammed into the tiny cell with me?

I knew life was unfair. I was not naïve enough to believe that there was any justice in the world. But at least I could hold on to some semblance of justice — to grasp at the illusion of fairness.

I had never been so uncomfortable. I wanted to fade away into vapor; shrink and slide between the metal bars that held me captive; run off into the night and to never be seen again. But there was no escape. Sleep was my only refuge. I found a spot against the farthest wall and told my mind to let go and drift away.

As I let my eyelids drop, an odor wafted through the air that was so vile, it was worse than the smell of death. Everyone noticed one-by-one. It caused an uproar in the cell. It was a man using the toilet. I couldn't understand why my life had come to this and where it was going. The rude man flushed, but it did little to bring relief. It encouraged the other men to do the same. So, the next man sat down and added to the stench that was already choking the life out of everyone in the jail.

Suddenly, the CO came to the cell and banged on the metal bars.

"Hey, you degenerate!" he shouted. "That toilet only works once every half hour. If somebody else just used it, you have to hold it. Got it?"

The moans and groans from the men filled the room as they realized that they would have to live with whatever the second man deposited for the next thirty minutes. It was slow, sadistic torture.

I prayed for release or death. Slowly, the men were called as their cases were arraigned and new inmates took their place in the crowded putrid place. I tried to sleep once again. As my eyes closed and my thoughts floated down into sleep, I heard a loud slap. Another man who felt he could wait no longer sat on the toilet. The muscle head, tattooed man slapped him across the face.

The sound of the CO's nightstick scraping across the bars started me to my feet. "You got your pre-dinner show and aromatherapy. I guess you're ready for some food now."

He was holding a tray of baloney sandwiches. I looked around the room, sure that everyone in there was thinking exactly what he was thinking. Finally, the muscle man spoke up.

"Hey fool. You gotta sit there until you can flush. I don't want to smell your crap while I eat. You get up from that toilet, I'm gonna put your head in it."

The young men snickered in the corner and held their noses.

I slumped back down to the floor. This was a cruel and brutal hell. What had I gotten myself into? When would this nightmare end?

They had taken my watch. I could only guess at the time. The minutes felt like hours, and the hours were getting longer and longer. There was a small circular window high up in the ceiling, no larger than a man's head. It was my only window to the outside. I glanced up to see if it held any clue about what time it was, but there were only stars wrapped in the darkness of night.

As time passed, the cell became more and more silent. Only one man, one of the young ones, had fallen asleep. His snoring was the only sound that broke the silence, except for the occasional noises coming from the officer's station on the other side of the locked door that led to this cell of horror.

I wondered for a few moments why no one was speaking anymore. Then it hit me. Phone calls. No one had been offered the chance to make any phone calls. Then a greater shock hit me. I had not been given a phone call either. Why had no one come to bail me out? I fantasized for a moment that, on the other side of the door, my loved ones were talking to the police and making arrangements for my release. But that was just a fantasy. The occasional laughter that seeped under the threshold let me know that no serious business was taking place over there. I was lost. I was alone. I was abandoned . . . at least for now.

Then a greater fear consumed me. If they had come to offer me a chance to call, whom would I call? They had taken my phone when they took my watch, wallet, and other belongings. No one memorized phone numbers anymore. I could not think of a single number. I racked my brain trying to remember or at least visualize a number on my screen—numbers I had seen a million times. This was not something I thought could ever happen to me. Sadness swept over me as I played out what the next hours might bring.

All at once, the guards came in and ordered everyone to get up and out of the cell. Like cattle, we were shuffled from the jail cell to a large holding room. Several other cells had been emptied as well. Of the forty to fifty men in the room, some looked dazed and confused. Others looked like they were hardened steel, having gone through this process too many times for any human soul to stand. I could easily pick out the first-timers. They looked like they had been shaken and were ready to wet their pants at any moment.

A large flat-screen television was positioned in front of the room and an even larger guard stood in front of it to address the inmates.

"OK, listen up! Hey, you, quiet down," he said pointing a nightstick at a man who seemed agitated. "In a few moments, we are going to call you up one by one. You will have a chance to speak to the judge. Some of you will be going home. Others won't. So, pay attention and listen for your name. And stay quiet while others are being arraigned."

I felt my heart sink. We were being spoken to like animals. Where was the grace? Where was the kindness? Where was the presumption of innocence? Nothing was redeeming about this process. On the contrary, it seemed designed specifically to break the spirit in two.

By this time, I was already dressed in the ugly orange jumpsuit they had given me when they took my clothes. All my possessions, including my clothing, had been stripped away. They had strip-searched me to be sure I was not carrying any weapons. They had done everything possible to dehumanize me.

The television screen came to life like a monster threatening to devour everyone in the room. The judge appeared on the screen. I could hear the men making predictions about who was going to be sent home and who would stay. I silently predicted (or hoped) my name would be called, the judge would say it was all a big mistake, and I would be sent home.

When I heard my name, the sound of it startled me. I jumped to my feet making the men in the room snicker. I walked up to the screen and heard words that changed my life forever. I was being sent to the "fourth floor." I did not know at the moment what it meant, but the sound of hoots and groans from the other men told me it wasn't good. The guard explained that I was being taken to the maximum-security area.

Some guys did not understand the process. I was one of them. It wasn't clear why anything that was happening was happening. I was subjected to a second strip search which included going deep into my body cavities. I was forced to spread my cheeks and cough so that anything placed in there could be discovered. Uncomfortable is not the right word for it. It was horrifying. I just prayed for it to be over. But, it was only beginning. A new level of horrors was about to unfold.

When you get to the end of all the
light you know and it's time to step
into the darkness of the unknown,
faith is knowing that one of two things
shall happen: either you will be given
something solid to stand on, or you
will be taught how to fly.

— EDWARD TELLER

CHAPTER 4

NEVER SURRENDER

September 2013

If you've never been violated or oppressed in the way that jail life can violate and oppress, it is hard to imagine how soul-sucking it can be. This was my first experience in the system. I had no idea such things were taking place behind the cold, grey walls of the correctional facility.

There were some men there, though, whose faces bore the scars of being locked up repeatedly. They didn't look like the other men. They didn't look like me. It wasn't just that their faces were cold and hard. It was everything about them. It was the way they walked and talked, even the way they breathed. I watched them draw in their breaths like it was a labor to be alive. They were weighted in their movements as if they were carrying the pain of their experiences like a heaviness they could hardly bear. I was surprised to see them laugh and smile. The first-timers never cracked so much as a grin. But even the smiles and laughter of the career convicts carried the heaviness of their grief at a life lost to the correctional system.

I did not want that for myself. I could not imagine what it was going to be like to have these walls close in on me. What would it be like to breathe the air in these air-conditioned rooms that circulated the devastating regret and darkness of spirit we were all feeling?

Even the guards seemed to have a cold and heavy look to them. They had seen things no human ever should. The only way they could manage to survive, it seemed, was to grow as mean, distant, and heartless as possible. So, their words were gruff and edgy. Their demeanor was defensive and barren. It was a cesspool that infected everyone. Even the judges, clerks, and lawyers were infected with the sickness of the soul that the *system* fostered.

I listened and observed, surprised by some of the conversations I heard. Some men seemed more content inside than out. They weren't happier by any means. Happiness was not a concept that existed in this space. But the familiarity of life inside seemed to be a comfort to them. I heard them speak about their responsibilities and the people who were living life without them on the outside. I could not tell if they were content to escape those responsibilities or if they were so damaged and broken by their experiences that they felt unable to face them. Either way, committing crimes was easy for them because jail had become a way of life.

They could sit in jail, be fed each day, and their lives would have the routine they desperately craved. There was a lot to wonder about. But there was one thing I never questioned: I did not belong there. I was not one of them. I did not identify with a single human being in the building, from the convicts to the judge. I was meant to have a life that was rich and full. I wondered if the key to my survival might be a refusal to surrender. That's when I decided that I would never surrender. Whatever was happening to me, I would not surrender the happiness, the freedom, the lightness of life free of the heavy burden of incarceration. *Never surrender!*

I looked over and saw a man enter. For the first time, I let out the breath I had been holding for 24 hours. It was my attorney. He was a good friend and a great lawyer. I did not know how he got there, who had called him, and how he knew when to appear. But like a faithful friend, there he was.

He shook my hand and pulled me in for a brief hug. I sat down in a haze. Everything around me seemed to tingle and I was in a surreal, alternative world. The real me was at home watching television drinking a beer and laughing with my family. This life I was watching was not real. It couldn't be.

The sound of my friend's voice shook me from my daydream and brought me back to the terrifying realness of the situation I was in.

"I saw the footage on television."

"Television," I asked in disbelief. "I was on television."

"Well, the helicopters that were there were police choppers, but there was also a news chopper. The reports they are giving are pretty bad. But I know you are innocent. I've known you long enough to know that you did not do the things they are saying on the air. We just have to figure out a way to prove it."

"What happens now? When do I get out of here?"

"Listen, take my advice. Don't think about getting out. It is just going to drive you crazy. If it happens, great. But don't go there. Let's just focus on getting these charges dropped. I'm here to represent you."

"What is this going to cost me?"

He slid a contract across the table to me. As I read it, my heart sank. Even if I won, I would be destitute. I would be starting my life over financially and in many other ways.

At my first court appearance, I stood and listened as the charges filed against me were read into the record. The bailiff could have been speaking Swahili for all I knew. The charges sounded like a foreign language. I recognized the words, of course. But the crimes that were attached to them were so heinous, those words could not possibly apply to me. I was dumbstruck! I wondered who could have done such things and how anyone could think that it could be me. Nothing was making sense. They were piling mounds and mounds of garbage on my head until I was buried.

Sixteen charges were read. Like sixteen sharp daggers, they pierced through my heart. Like sixteen heavy anvils, they fell from the sky and crushed my soul. Like sixteen little-death sentences, they threatened to take my life away. It was David. And the sixteen charges were my Goliath. If I did not fight, I would surely die.

I was placed on the list of the 50 most dangerous criminals in jail. Me! I had been betrayed by someone. My emotions were running on high. Suddenly, I felt my fear subside and a new emotion took its place: anger. I was furious. I had to find out who was responsible for this and bring them down. I was a victim, but I refused to be helpless. Someone had set me up. And they were going to pay.

My mind started to drift into a dark place. I did not ask for this. I did not cause this. But this was no accident. Someone caused this and the universe allowed it. God had turned his back on me, or so I thought. All the plans that were set for my life had been summarily canceled. I was going someplace with my life before all of this came upon me. I had a future. I had a destiny. But at that moment, it seemed that all I had were sixteen charges that taunted me and promised to take it all away.

The darkness was creeping in. It was starting to cloud my vision and break my heart into pieces. I couldn't be sure, but I thought that the darkness was so ominous and so strong, that it would control me forever. I could not let that happen. I had to find a way to fight it. I decided that the best way to combat the darkness was to bring in the light. And the place that needed the light the most was staring me in the face. These false charges would wither under the strength of the light. I just needed to find that light.

I wanted to understand everything that was happening. I wanted to become an expert in everything that was going on. So, I decided to become a student of the legal system. I would not simply let this all happen to me. I would know as much as I could about every aspect of the legal system.

I've always questioned myself and challenged myself. I was never one to back down from a challenge. I searched for ways to better myself in everything I did. And whatever I was working on at the time, I would give it my all. That mental attitude would be critical if I was going to survive here. This would be my biggest challenge.

Things were about to get even more interesting for me. I had fallen silent as I listened to the judge and the lawyer converse. The judge, who was supposed to represent the symbol of fairness, seemed annoyed. He wanted to rush through the process and get on with his next case. I realized a terrible truth, that the system I was now locked in saw everyone as a group. I was not an individual. I was not a unique man with family, friends, joys, fears, talents, weaknesses, successes, and failures. I was part of the blob that they called criminals. Everyone in that room who was dressed in orange was looked at the same way. We were nameless, faceless, and lifeless to the people on the other side of the bench. Even though I was innocent, I was viewed in the same way as everyone else in the room. And I would be treated the same, as well. I needed to become stronger than I had ever been and I needed to do it quickly! There was no time to waste.

I decided that I would keep my head. I would understand this all. It was foreign to me now, but if I kept my head, I would learn it. I would conquer. But keeping my head was no easy task. My mind frequently tried to wander and drift away. I began to doubt my memory. Some moments were so surreal, I began to question my sanity. *Maybe I blacked out and did something I don't know about or don't remember. Could they be right? They seem so certain that they have the right man. Could it have been me and I just don't recall it?* But then I shook my head and reminded myself that I was innocent and needed to defend that innocence.

I could feel the bitterness creeping up from my toes. I worried that I was losing it all. A week before, I could reach out and hug my children whenever I wanted to. I regretted every moment I failed to seize and treasure. I began to think about the beauty of nature that I could not go outside and enjoy. I had been chasing paper and wasting the precious moments of life. And now I had lost those moments.

The charges were heinous. I could not imagine how anyone could do such things, much less how I could. They believed that I had killed people and stuffed their lifeless bodies in body bags. I was made to look like a homicidal terrorist. Since the guards and judges did not know if I was the killer, I was treated as if I was the killer. My innocence no longer mattered. I had to sink into this new role that I was not prepared for. I had no one to turn to.

I had always known that life was filled with lessons; they were everywhere and in everything. There was also some nugget of wisdom that could come from a situation, no matter how terrible it was. I had practiced the art of learning from life, getting better, and overcoming obstacles. This would be the greatest test of my efforts.

I was not the vicious guy the prosecutor portrayed me to be. However, his description was so vile and brutal, my fame spread throughout the jail. As I was escorted—bound at my hands and feet—to the cell I would be calling home for the next several weeks, months, or years, I noticed that I was not alone. One man was sitting on the top bunk, another man was in the cell resting on the bottom bunk, and a third and fourth man was sitting on the floor against the wall. The man on the bottom bunk nodded to me as I walked in. I shot him a look. He jumped up and got down on the floor. I walked over and sat on the bottom bunk realizing for the first time that my name had become somewhat legendary in the halls. But this was nothing to be proud of. It only terrified me more.

> You can't help getting older, but you don't have to get old.
>
> — GEORGE BURNS

I can only imagine what my demeanor was. I knew the rage I was feeling inside. But it was pouring out of my insides and showing up on my face. It was a warning to everyone that I was not to be messed with. I was determined that I was not going to be sleeping on the floor. Someone else would have that. If I was going to be perceived as tough, I had to believe that I was and behave that way. Otherwise, this environment would swallow me whole. There would be nothing left of me when this ordeal was over.

I was in a new environment, and I had to make the appropriate adjustments. I saw things in those early days that changed me fundamentally. I watched two men spark an argument that happened so fast, it was like lightning. They went from talking to complete fury. One man picked up his tray and beat the other man senseless. He was bloody and knocked out cold before the guard even had time to take his first step toward the commotion. That was the way things worked on the inside. Everything that happened was at a different level. Time moved differently. The cramped conditions brought out the worst in every human.

And there I was, right in the thick of it. It would test my mettle and make me prove all of the philosophies I had used to live my life. If what I had come to know about life was true, it would be tested in this environment.

Life is filled with unanswered questions, but it is the courage to seek those answers that continues to give meaning to life. You can spend your life wallowing in despair, wondering why you were the one who was led towards the road strewn with pain, or you can be grateful that you are strong enough to survive it.

— J.D. STROUBE,
  CAGED BY DAMNATION

CHAPTER 5

QUESTIONS

October 2013

Over time, the men in jail started to call me Dread. I heard it was because of the dreadful demeanor of my resting face. It sparked fear and terror in their hearts. They had no idea what I was capable of. I liked it that way and made sure to live up to the reputation I was building.

There were many different ways of coping with the craziness that was life in jail. A man could let it break him so that he was only a shell of his former self when he was finally freed. Some let it harden them and turn them into stone. They were good for nothing but the jail walls when their time was served. They usually ended up back in the system before too long. Then there were people like me: actors. I was playing a role. I refused to believe that this was real because, if it were, it would destroy the best parts of me and erode my very soul. So I played the role.

I made daily adjustments to survive the dark places. In no time, I was respected and accepted into society. Guys would bring me the canteens of other guys so that I would have one. This was their way of giving me gifts. It was the currency of incarceration. After some time, I urged them to stop taking canteens from some guys and giving them to me. It wasn't who I wanted to be.

Day in and day out, I could feel my anger grow because I did not feel that I was making progress. I finally got my phone call. I called someone who could put money on my jail account so that I could buy the things I needed once per week. I was able to buy things like food, cigarettes, and supplies. It was an awakening to learn how things work behind the walls of the jail.

I was in the fight of my life. Things were uncertain. Since I did not know who my enemy was, everyone became my enemy. Time stopped moving in years or months. It moved day by day. My thirst for revenge was churning within me. Someone had done this to me. Someone had to pay. All the while, I tried to keep a sane mind behind the cold, hateful walls. Those walls squeezed the life out of me. They taunted me and threatened to never let me go. I couldn't move. I couldn't breathe. And I had no clear exit strategy.

Why am I here, I asked. *What am I supposed to learn? What am I supposed to do?* I knew there was a lesson in all of this, but my mind was racing and I could not control it. I imagined every alternate possibility. *What could I have done differently to make sure I was not in this situation? What moves could I make?*

I questioned everything about my life. That is what jail will do for you. It makes you doubt every move you have made, from the time you were old enough to make choices. I even questioned how I had spent so much time chasing women. How many different women could I have? It had been one of the most important things to me. That was my focus.

Sitting in jail, I realized that I had wasted so many years with the wrong attitude and foolish thinking. I could have spent those years in a committed relationship with someone I loved and together we could have been on a journey making a life. Would I ever have that now? I had spent some of the best years of my life luring women into my life and my bed. I told them what they wanted to hear, and they trusted me. But was I worthy of their trust? Or had I become just another predator out to get what he wanted?

My life became all about the missed opportunities, bad decisions, and painful regrets that haunted me like ghosts. I could not find myself because I was deep inside my head. I was overthinking every breath I breathed. I could have made some major moves that would have put me in a better position. Now that I was in chains, literally and figuratively, what would the future hold?

I had spent my life disrupting. I was prone to steal someone's girlfriend. I carried a gun. I did not ever shy away from a fight. I was not afraid to confront anyone about anything. If someone stole from me or from someone I loved, they would face the wrath only I knew how to bring. I was also the life of the party. I never missed the weekend fun of parties and bar hopping. Then, when we left the party, I would drive through the city in the middle of the night with my music blasted at its full power. I shook the walls and the ground of the neighborhoods I passed through, and I did not care who I disturbed. And no one had the right to say anything to me about it or they might get an earful back. I was a disrupter. Now, though, my life had been disrupted. And I didn't like it at all.

I could look back and see that my priorities had been misplaced. How could I have been so blind? I was more concerned about the car I drove than the person I was becoming. I bought expensive rims to put on the wheels of my car. I made sure the rims spun hard and fast so that everyone I passed could see them. The irony is that I hardly ever saw them spin because I was driving the car. From the inside, the rims were not visible. That was such a powerful lesson to me of how I lived for the world and not for myself. I lived for what was "out there" instead of living for what was inside of me.

This was real. I would have to live inside myself now. And it was loud and dark and scary inside of my head. In this place of confinement, I had time to reflect. I was like a sheep being moved from one place to the next. I knew that I had to outsmart the criminals who were in jail with me.

I had to be better, smarter, wiser, faster, and stronger than them all.

I had no respect for my fellow inmates. I saw myself as being far above them. In some ways, that might have been true. After all, I heard their stories. I heard how they committed their crimes and left enough evidence to sink a ship or stayed in one place too long after robbing it so that they were easy to catch.

Many of them hurt their cases with their testimony. Some of them were high on drugs and went through a pharmacy to rob the drugstore. They sat there in the drugstore waiting for the person at the register to hand them the drugs. I couldn't imagine how anyone could be so foolish. They didn't cover their faces, so not only was the person they were robbing an eyewitness to their identity but they were being filmed on the store's surveillance camera. They handed the cashier a note with their fingerprints and in their handwriting. They sat in the drive-through which was a confined area making it easy for police cruisers to block them in on every side. Often they compounded their crimes by hurting civilians or attacking the police.

These were some of the stupid crimes I heard about on the inside. The crimes were dumb, the criminals were dumb. It was not hard for me to rise to the top of the criminal class. I decided that I would take advantage of my intellect. I would even try to have some fun with it.

There were certain privileges we were offered. Once per week, we would get something decent to eat. The food most days was not fit for a pig. It was slop they threw together as cheaply as they possibly could. It was not like eating in a five-star restaurant.

The best meals were the ones with beans. They were at least edible. So, I looked forward to that once-weekly meal where food would be prepared that was a bit better, tastier, and more appealing to the eye. On chicken days, I was determined to get the chicken away from as many people as I could. I would offer protection to the smaller guys who were tired of constantly getting beat up. The only way they could pay me was to give me their chicken. One plate of food would buy them my services for the week. I would have half a dozen chickens on my plate on Fridays.

The guys who were not foolish criminals were either mentally ill or suffering the effects of years of drug use. The jail system had no regard for people who were high when they were arrested. They were not sent to rehab to get well. They were sent to jail. And, in most cases, they did not have the benefit of any soft place to land when they came down from their drug of choice. They fell fast and they fell hard. Many of them went into withdrawal and had severe side effects from stopping the drugs so abruptly. It made them easy to manipulate and control.

One man was brought into jail asleep. He was carried in and placed in his cell. He did not wake up for four days. The jail officials didn't even care enough to get him any medical attention. They seemed thankful that they had one less "animal" to think about. When he woke up, he went into a panic. He did not know where he was or what had happened to him. He did not remember anything that had happened over the previous days, so he lost his mind when he realized where he was. He did not know what crimes he had committed. It was as if he were outside of his body and completely out of his mind.

I learned that, in that space, there was no life. If I was going to have a life, I was going to have to make it.

I say that there is no life on the inside. It is true both figuratively and literally. The people are slowly dying as they watch their youth and their vitality slipping away. There are no hopes and dreams. You don't hear anyone talking about goals and strategies for when they leave jail. It is a hard life that is mostly dead. But, quite literally, there is no life. You hardly ever see a bug. One day, a mosquito flew over someone's head. No one dared to kill it. It was like a sighting of the Pope. It was sacred. People began to talk about how there must be a crack or a hole somewhere in the walls. For days and days, people talked about it. It dominated all our conversations. People spent their days and nights searching for it. We never found it. But it was exciting.

I watched this all unfold. This was a new way of living. I knew that if I was going to survive, I would have to be like the mosquito except I would have to find my way out. I would have to continue dreaming, wishing, hoping, and planning. I would have to embrace life daily or, over time, I would start to look, act, and think like those around me.

One day, the power in the jail went out. In a maximum-security jail, a power outage is a major crisis. The jail goes into lockdown. Some people tried to escape but none of them even came close. It hit me when those lights went out that other people ran to their cells. It had become their safe space. I froze. It was as if everything around me went silent. Even though inmates were running, guards were yelling, and people were clanging metal doors, it was all white noise that faded into the background.

Amid pure blackness all around me, there was suddenly a bright light ahead. The light was moving toward me. I knew that it was going to consume me. It wrapped me in warmth. I felt the energy. I felt life. I heard a voice say, "You have a purpose. It is greater than your fulfillment." It was the most beautiful moment I had ever experienced. I was awash with peace. My mind rested. Images of my family flashed before me. I could see myself in the future pursuing a career. Everything was in perspective.

> Cage an eagle and it will bite at the wires, be they of iron or of gold.
>
> — HENRIK IBSEN,
> *THE VIKINGS OF HELGELAND*

CHAPTER 6

WORK IT OUT

November 2013

The light had come to me and It had shown me my future. It had brought me life, promising me that these days would pass and brighter days lay ahead. I was so sure of what I saw and felt that I began to act on it. I realized that my only task was to become what I had seen.

It was time for me to address the elephant in the room. It was time for me to carve my path going forward. I had some chinks in my armor. I was not a knight, but I wanted to be one. The way I had lived my life up to that point had not worked. But the light had renewed me and brought me a world of possibility. I stopped saying "If I get out." I changed my conversation to say, "When I get out." The power of my confession helped me to know that these dark days would end. I had seen the light.

I had no idea when I would get out. From a legal perspective, nothing was looking good. The court case was not progressing well. Everything in the natural world threatened to stop me from going on with the best parts of my life. These were dark hours. But the light had come, and I held on to what I had seen. My faith grew strong. I believed.

I started setting goals in this uncomfortable place. Since the guys in jail looked up to me, I decided to step into my role as a leader. I asked myself what I could do to bring light into their dark places. The answers came and I started teaching them chess, card games, and checkers. We shared laughs. It gave them something to move towards.

This whole experience was happening so that I could understand the light. I started to read and study everything to understand this spiritual experience. I had a lot to do: children to care for, to show that I loved them and that I was here for them. I had to be their dad. Jail could not take that from me. What I was learning in jail could be put to use. This time did not have to be wasted. It could be useful.

The light continued to speak to me. It was telling me what I needed to do. I asked. "Who am I?"

The light said, "You are beautiful. You are a man with a dream. Your sons want to look up to you. They want to be proud of you. They want to show you off. Teach them how to envision a dream and bring that dream to life."

It seemed as if I woke up in that moment of seeing the light. I had been asleep in a nightmare. It was a horrific dream that had captured my mind. Now I was awake.

Stepping into the light, however, brought great challenges and responsibilities. Was I ready? Would I be a storyteller? Would I be a motivator? Would I be a leader? I had so much to bring to the table. I was intelligent and had run a company with a six-figure income. Now it was time to put it all to use. I felt compromised by my situation. But it was time to stop my focus on the confinement, on the bars, on the locks. The light kept on speaking:

- You can do this.
- Your life is ahead.
- You will understand eventually.
- You will learn lessons from all you have been through.
- Let me shine my light on those dark places.

I asked myself, *How do I let the light guide me?* But the light replied,

I don't need to guide you. I just need to light the path you will walk. You already have everything within that you need to make it! And as you go, you will hold the light within you. It will radiate out to all those around you. You will light up every dark place along the way. You are a man on a mission. You are a man with a dream.

I realized that all the paths had been dark. They were dark paths or wrong paths, they were paths devoid of light. Now that the light had come, the paths were all lit and bright, and beautiful. I could walk down any one of them and find happiness and great success. I possessed the light within myself. I would become the light and bring it to others, just as the light was brought to me. I decided at that moment that no matter what came my way, no matter what people said, no matter what the courts decided, I was going to be OK. I was going to make it, and I remembered a great spiritual truth spoken by Iyanla Vanzant,

No storm can last forever. It will never rain for 365 days consecutively. Keep in mind that trouble comes to pass, not to stay. Don't worry! No storm, not even the one in your life, can last forever.

CHAPTER 7

THE STORMS DONE COME

December 2013

When I was young, a hurricane swept over my island. It destroyed everything it touched. There is no way to describe what it feels like to be in the middle of a hurricane. At one point, it picked me up and threatened to toss me across a field. I was only saved because I reached out for a railing and held on with all my might. I was blowing sideways with my legs in the air. It was terrifying. When the hurricane ended, there was a calm blue sky and the beautiful light of the sun shone down on my home. The worst moment of my childhood was followed by the most beautiful moment.

The same was true of my ordeal in jail. I was in a major storm that was throwing me all over the place. It had destroyed the life that I had known. But if I could hold on for a few minutes, a few more days, a few more months, I would be on the other side where the birds were singing and the sun was shining again.

There is so much in life we cannot control. Yet, we try so hard to control those uncontrollable things. We feel a sense of loss, helplessness, and hopelessness when we cannot control them. When we cannot control our circumstances, we must focus on the things that we can do. My life behind bars was temporary. I was ready to think big and I was filled with hope. I combined that hope with all of the gifts that I had been given. My faith was strong, and I was ready to use everything I had to succeed, survive, and overcome. The universe would bring me what I wanted.

I saw all the things that were not going my way. There was a setback and after setback. But I decided to release them. It was time to move into a new phase. There were things I needed to handle in a better way. I aligned myself with everything inside. The Leo within stood up on his hind legs and began to roar. Now it was time for the doing. I committed to being persistent in everything I did. I wanted to make my mark on the world and have an impact on my children. I wanted my journey to mean something and have significance far beyond my years.

Depression tried its best to creep in from time to time. It tried to block the light. I was out of my mind with worry on some days. I could take my own life before anyone could stop me. Would I give in to that pain and helplessness? No! I knew that I was going to be OK if I focussed on the light. The darkness was just space - a void filled with irritation, lack of motivation, frustration, and anger. It promised to take me nowhere. But with the light, I knew that I had a chance. Because I focussed on it, the light wrapped itself around my life.

I was in jail with guys who were serving multiple life sentences. They were hard men who had no chance of experiencing life outside ever again. They had become career criminals and it showed. The light showed me a better life. I did not have to be like them. But I was facing 32 years to life. Just as their paths appeared dark, my path appeared dark as well. I was fighting a political system, a cultural system, and the justice system.

They needed to heal and I needed to heal. I had to shine the light on my life and not be afraid of people seeing who I was. I couldn't save everyone in jail. But since the light found me, I had a responsibility to shine the light inside the jail. I began to volunteer my time so that I could give back, and I committed to volunteering when I got out of jail as well. The men in jail told me what a difference I was making in their lives. It was my way of reclaiming the sanity that jail life can take away.

I decided I would write a play. But to do that, I needed to spend some hours studying. I needed to read so that I could offer the best play possible to those who would see it. The librarian felt I was making a difference. He supported me and brought me armloads of books so I could study. Once I finished writing the play, the librarian continued to encourage me to read and to write.

I think back on some of the blessings that came to me during that period and realize that I did not deserve any of them. I think back to how frustrated I was when I was doing time in jail. My life was very challenging. The hardest part was seeing what it did to others around me because I knew that it could do the same thing to me. There were several guys in each cell. I felt this was inhuman and it made me angry.

I didn't get to ask questions when I needed to. I had to just live with my questions. Living with questions is like living in a private hell. The questions haunt you and make you feel as if you are slipping away from reality. I was making such good progress within myself. But on the outside, I had no answers. I did not know when I would be leaving. I did not receive any kind of regular updates on my case. It was terrifying. It was enough to scare the life out of a man.

As a father, my heart continued to reach out for my boys. I thought about them all of the time. I was able to silence my anxious thoughts about most things, but when it came to my children, I could not quiet my mind. *Where were they? What were they doing? What were they thinking? How were they dealing with missing me? Were they sad, and who was there to comfort and reassure them?* My father's heart could not be consoled. So, I decided to let the light shine on that dark place as well. I realized that I took my time with them for granted. When I was on the outside, I could see them, hug them, hang out with them, and play with them anytime I wanted to. Now that I was inside, there was a new value to that time. I swore an oath that I would never take that time for granted again. That is what the light of truth does.

I had this place in my mind where I had to think of all my relationships. I decided that I would be far more cautious about whom I would let into my space once I was a free man. I had wasted so much time with people who did not deserve my time. When I started to interact with the people on the outside again, I would be more careful. When you are vulnerable, people who don't have your best interests at heart will take advantage of you. They will use you and waste your time. Time is the one thing we can never get back. Losing time is what jail is all about. It is the greatest punishment one human being can impose upon another. It is worse than death. At least with death, time stops. But when you are serving time, the seconds on the clock tick more and more slowly and torture your mind.

All in all, I spent ten months in that dark place. But I did not know that it would be ten months. It felt like a lifetime and there was no end in sight. When it did end, it ended suddenly and without warning.

Anger was standing by the door of the cell asking if it could walk with me that day. It was up to me to refuse anger as a companion. Suicide was also there wooing me to give up on this life and leave it altogether. I had to fight to reject it as well. Then despair stepped forward and asked for permission to live in my thoughts. It warned me that I would be ruined for society when I got out. It tried to tell me that no one would love me, trust me, or connect with me again. I rejected its lies as well.

> Every person needs an adventure to chase, a dragon to slay, and somebody to save.
>
> — JOHN ELDREDGE

The light was always there beckoning to me to turn away from the darkness. It was a struggle. But each day, I reached for the light and we walked together throughout the day. The fight was on and I was clinging to the light day by day. No matter what my situation was, I needed to remember that God had sent me that light.

Many people don't believe in God. But I know that the universe hears when we speak. I was speaking to God, who was my universe, and I received the strength each day to keep going and not give up. I was grateful that the light found me. The darkness could no longer damage or assault me. I would be free. I would be strong. I would be whole.

CHAPTER 8

STEPPING INTO PURPOSE

Winter 2014

So many people never get to step into their purpose. Their lives are lived on autopilot. They simply follow their desires around like an obedient slave. When they are hungry, they eat. When they are tired, they sleep. When they want sexual pleasure, they seek out unsuspecting partners. These are low-resolution people who live in the lowest order of humanity. They do not know their purpose, so they cannot walk in it. They have no thought about the greater good.

Their lives are lived for themselves. They have no light to shine on their situation, so they cannot shine the light on others.

But we are all called upon to live by a higher law and shine a light on the dark places. The more people living in the light, the less darkness there will be. The world will be brighter because of it. When your brother or sister has an encounter with the light, it just means that the light is spreading across the globe. We can all contribute to the community, to life, to love. We all have a part to play. Darkness brings chaos. It causes us to retreat into a safe place. But our safe places aren't really safe. They are just familiar. In reality, our dark places are cold, they are hard to navigate, and they are lonely. A spot in the light is a blessing to all because you can uplift those around you. The light you shine on others shows them that their life has value and purpose. The light helps them to discover it and walk in it.

Life is a team sport. None of us are lone rangers. We call ourselves individuals. Yet, we were not designed to live as individuals. We were designed to live in a community and connect. We cannot just shine our light on others. We must also teach them to find and share the light. Then everyone has an opportunity to step into their purpose.

When I was a young boy, I always heard people talk about being in a dark place. I had no idea what they meant by that. Once I reached the depths of that awful place, I understood. Just as the light had found me, the darkness had found me first. I had put myself in a situation where I was exposed. What life had to offer me looked very good on the surface. So I allowed it to consume me. There were no immediate consequences. Everything seemed to be going my way. But darkness is insidious. In time, the darkness exacts a price. Like a bill that had come due, it demanded to be paid and the price was my life and my freedom. I ignored the darkness for too long, and it grew and grew, until it was a monster.

My foundation was not stable, so everything that came my way blew me and tossed me. My foundation needed to be firm and solid. It needed to be built with the light so that I would always be secure. The best thing about the light is that it gives you the ability to see clearly. I cannot stress enough how critical it is to be able to see clearly, from both a physical and a spiritual perspective. People who see clearly can navigate their way around obstacles. They can make good moves because their sight is clear. They have a vision. Their vision for the future is bright. They can pay attention to details. They are less apt to make mistakes. The light is effective. It is powerful.

As I sat in the jail, I remembered many times when I had relied on GPS to get me where I needed to go. It was a great luxury because it alerted me to construction, roadblocks, traffic, accidents, etc. That GPS function is essentially like shining a light on the path to our destination.

Sometimes in life, though, the fastest route is not the best one. It is so easy to take the shortcuts in life because they seem like a fast track to the things we want. Yet, when we take that shortcut, we may discover that it gets us off track and leads us to a place we do not want to be. Worse, that place could very well be difficult to leave. Once we wise up and try to get back on the right path, it may be tough to find. There have been times when I was driving and tried to avoid a slowdown, only to find that I wasted more time trying to get around than I would have spent if I had just stayed on the path.

Some roads we take in life are just risky. We have to understand that there is a path that is most fitting for us. The light helped me see that. It became the best kind of GPS because the light made all the roads clear. I could finally see clearly. All of my decisions became easier to make. I was able to take what I knew and run with it.

Nothing in my life was wasted. I had embraced purpose. Going forward, I would use everything I had learned and experienced on my journey. The key, of course, was persistence. I could not even entertain the possibility of quitting. I had to show the universe that I was serious about my promise to make something out of this precious life it had given me. I would return the gifts I had received. I would plant them like seeds in a field and watch them sprout and grow. I would choose the path that would bring me to the highest and greatest expression of myself. I would grow into the person the light showed me I could be.

Of course, there would be challenges, adversity. But I had to adjust my thinking about those challenges. I had seen them as my enemy. Now, I realized that the challenges were there to grow me as an individual. They were my fuel. They would rocket me from where I was to where I needed to be.

All I needed to do was hang on because changing your life can be a bumpy ride.

Despite the anger, the pain, the confusion, the doubt, and the fear, there was always something I could learn. My next move was bound to be my best move. I was properly positioned to fail, but I was also properly positioned to succeed. Why? I had lost it all in the incarceration. I had the option of giving up. I could let the jail swallow me. I could give up the fight for justice and freedom. I could surrender my future. Or, I could look at this as my lowest point and realize that there was nowhere to go but up. I had been torn down like a condemned building. So, I could use this crisis to my advantage. I could build a strong foundation this time—one that would stand the test of time and support the great, big, amazing life I was preparing to build. What would make my foundation strong? The light. God. These are the things to build a foundation upon.

It was all about the journey now. Nothing I had done in the past had worked. But it was now all a part of my toolkit. The bad things in my past would now become my lessons in what not to do. All the good in my past would now become my partners on the journey. How could I better myself? How could I prove that I was worthy of the chance to move forward? How could I earn the chance that the light was giving to make it right? These were the questions I began to ask myself. I was determined to succeed!

We are all consumed by something. It is unavoidable. We can be consumed by darkness or light. We can be consumed by joy or despair. We can be consumed by purpose or hopelessness. For the first time, I was thinking clearly. The negativity was losing strength. Yes, my situation was bad. But I was here. I had to make the best of a bad situation. It was my turn to contribute to the greater good and make my life a gift to the world. I could be a producer rather than a consumer.

Beautiful things can emerge from dark places. Seeds can germinate in the dark and emerge to reach for the sun as they grow into the most beautiful plants, flowers, or trees. Photographers develop their pictures in the dark. When they are done, they turn on the light to illuminate the beautiful picture they took. Babies are held in the darkness of the womb, where their bodies are formed and perfected. Then they break free from that darkness and emerge into a bright and beautiful world. Such was the case for me. I had been in the dark. I had been broken and reshaped. I had been developed and formed. I had been nourished and challenged. Now, it was time for me to emerge because the light had come to me.

The possibilities were limitless for me. I could show society that I belonged. I was no longer a taker, but a giver. It may sound cliché, but I would make the world a better place. With that big, bold mission as my major goal in life, I was sure the universe would assist me. It would not be easy. I would have to summon the greatest stores of courage within me. I would have to be brave in the face of some big, bad dragons. I would have to battle the demons within my own heart and soul. They would have to be slain first.

Additionally, I would have to battle the justice system to prove my innocence and be freed. Then I would have to battle the fear of going back out into the world, declaring that I am a new man to my family and friends who might not believe that I could be changed. I would have to battle society as a whole that lumped all convicts in one group and considered them all to be wasted humanity. I would, with the help of the universe, conquer it all. Did I know how? No. All I had was the light and my goals. But that was all I needed.

I looked back at my childhood. I know that my childhood self had not interacted with my adult self. They were connected because one led to the other. I needed to integrate that young boy from the past with the man I saw in the mirror. I needed to become whole with all parts of myself. I could not afford to leave anything behind. That young me could help gown-up me. Even though he was a child, he was full of hope and wonder. He was bright-eyed and full of joy. He had virtually no fears. He believed that he could do anything. That is the magic and beauty of youth. It is not encumbered with the limitations adults take on as they get older.

My young self was not questioning himself and doubting his abilities. He thought he could leap tall buildings in a single bound. He thought he could run through brick walls. He took on any and every challenge. And if people doubted him, that made him want to prove them wrong. Their doubt was fuel to him. He could not be discouraged. I needed the energy and spirit that my younger self could bring me.

As I brought all parts of myself together, I began to experience a feeling of perfect peace. It washed over me like the cool, crispy waters of a forest stream. It soothed my soul and calmed my fears. It was a peace that I knew would last. It would be challenged by adversity, but it would endure. This life-changing peace was the final puzzle piece in my rebirth. I was delighted by the power it gave me.

For the first time, my anxious heart found relief. I was grateful for everything. I was grateful for my wonderful family — mostly for my sons. I was grateful for the air I breathed. I was grateful for my life. I was even grateful for the pain. I was grateful for the darkness because of what it had birthed in me. I was grateful for my enemies who had put me in this terrible place. What they meant to be my destruction would turn out to be my blessing and opportunity.

At some point, the struggle would be over. I did not know when that would be as I could not predict it. But I knew that it would come.

IF: A Father's Advice to His Son
by Rudyard Kipling

If you can keep your head when all about you
Are losing theirs and blaming it on you,
If you can trust yourself when all men doubt you,
But make allowance for their doubting too;

If you can wait and not be tired by waiting,
Or being lied about, don't deal in lies,

Or being hated, don't give way to hating,
And yet don't look too good, nor talk too wise

If you can dream - and not make dreams your master;
If you can think - and not make thoughts your aim;
If you can meet with Triumph and Disaster
And treat those two impostors just the same;

If you can bear to hear the truth you've spoken
Twisted by knaves to make a trap for fools,
Or watch the things you gave your life to, broken,
And stoop and build 'em up with worn-out tools

If you can make one heap of all your winnings
And risk it on one turn of pitch-and-toss,
And lose, and start again at your beginnings
And never breathe a word about your loss;

If you can force your heart and nerve and sinew
To serve your turn long after they are gone,
And so hold on when there is nothing in you
Except for the Will which says to them: 'Hold on!'

If you can talk with crowds and keep your virtue,
Or walk with Kings - nor lose the common touch,
If neither foes nor loving friends can hurt you,
If all men count with you, but none too much;

If you can fill the unforgiving minute
With sixty seconds' worth of distance run,
Yours is the Earth and everything that's in it,
And - which is more - you'll be a Man, my son!

If you want to identify me, ask me
not where I live, or what I like to
eat, or how I comb my hair, but ask
me what I am living for, in detail,
ask me what I think is keeping me
from living fully for the thing I
want to live for.

— THOMAS MERTON

CHAPTER 9

WHERE IS YOUR HEAD?

Spring 2014

I was down to about 190 pounds. The food was so bad in the jail, it was not fit to eat. The one weekly special meal was the only one that came close to satisfying. I survived on chips and an occasional burrito. I was busy working behind the walls. But I wasn't eating. Having only 190 pounds on my 6-foot frame was cause for concern.

I laughed. Is this really how I was spending the precious days of my life? I did not know that something beautiful was sitting just over the horizon. I had been put into the ultimate darkness, and I assumed it would require the fight of my life to escape it. I thought it would be years before I was free. Nevertheless, I was ready to invest whatever time it took.

The bible stories and the life of Christ became an inspiration for me. He told the world that he was the light. Still, they took that light and put it in a tomb — the place of ultimate darkness. They rolled a stone in front of the tomb to ensure that the light would not be seen ever again. But the light could not be contained. In the darkness, he completed his greatest work and then burst forth for the world to see. Once he conquered that darkness, he would never be subjected to it again. Such is the case for you and me. If we can push through the darkness, the resulting light will shine so brightly that it can never again be contained.

I began to study other great leaders: heads of state, political forces, motivational leaders, and others. Some were evil and their hearts were filled with darkness. There was no good place for them. They had been completely consumed by the darkness; it had crushed anything of value within their souls. Others went into a dark place and emerged better and stronger despite (and because of) all they had been through. Even the darkness of death was not enough to keep them concealed. Martin Luther King Jr. was one of those people. He was pushed to the darkness of death. His enemies believed that if they killed him they would silence him. The opposite occurred. He became more powerful in death than he was in life. His message went from a local entreaty to a global movement. Fifty years later, his light shines brighter than it ever had during his lifetime.

The key for me, I felt, was to keep moving. There were days when I would take huge leaps forward. There were many more days when I barely moved an inch. But it did not matter whether I was going a mile or just one step; I knew that I had to keep moving. Failure was not an option, and I was determined to succeed.

Positive thinking became much more than some esoteric concept. It became tangible and real. In many ways, I felt like a hurdle jumper. As the starting pistol prepares to go off, the runners keep their heads down because they want to come out of the starting blocks with immediate intensity. Once they are at speed, they think about the next leg of their journey. They can see the hurdles in front of them. So, they set about timing their steps to reach each one and sail over it. One false move could slow them down. And a loss of speed could mean an inability to scale the next hurdle. The hurdles are a part of the race. A runner cannot simply say, "I want to run the race without hurdles." He or she cannot choose to remove the hurdles from the race. Each hurdle must be faced by each athlete. The beauty of hurdle jumpers is that, if you knock over a hurdle, you are not disqualified from the race. You can even still win the race. Life is the same. As you face hurdles, you may stumble and even fall. But as long as you don't give up, you are not disqualified. The charges against me threatened to disqualify me from life. But once I realized I was still in the race, I dug in and ran hard with all of my might.

During times of pain, I learned that I had to remember love. The light brought me a sense of love and being loved. It took love to bring the light to me: the love of God, the love of the universe. I was undeserving, but the light came to me anyway, maybe because I had been offered an important purpose. I knew that I could grow from that love, and I could be a conduit of that love to others. Maybe that was my purpose.

It is easy to love those who love you in return. And it is also easy to love the lovely. But some don't love us. They position themselves as enemies and critics. They don't return our love with love. Instead, they respond with hatred, jealousy, and strife. But that simply means that they are the ones most starved for the special kind of love that comes from someone who is in the light.

That was the love I wanted to spread. The light would not allow me to give anything less. Anything less would be untrue to whom I was becoming. I was going all-in with my new life. I would not give it part of me or half of my available effort. I threw my whole self into who I was becoming. I needed the universe to know that it chose well when it chose me.

Though the light might sometimes be obscured by circumstances, it cannot be extinguished, just like the sun cannot be seen when the clouds are covering it. We know that it is still there, shining its light. There is a dance that happens when light and darkness meet. The first one impacts how they play off each other. Each one serves its purpose in kind.

It helped that I remembered what it was like to live in the light of freedom. I did not know it at the time, but freedom was one of the greatest gifts God gave to humankind. Of course, it was not until I had lost that precious gift that I came to treasure it for what it is and all it provides. In some ways, I was lucky that I knew the difference between bondage and freedom. Millions of people on the other side of the wall did not know how to value the gift of life and freedom the way I could now. This was one more thing to be grateful for.

From time to time, my mind would drift back to those glorious days of liberty I once enjoyed. In my imagination, I returned to some of the places whose beauty and wonder were always there to be enjoyed. But we had been so busy with meetings, big deals, phone calls, and plans, we were unable or unwilling to see all they had to show us. In my mind, I returned to one river in particular where the water was so clear and clean, I could see to the bottom. The smell of the air was crisp and fresh; it almost had a taste. The water would not let me go. As a seductress, it kept beckoning me to come closer. It drove my fears away. There were no worries by the riverside. There was only peace and sweetness and the melody of the birds.

It was hard to leave this place in my mind. I wanted to stay there forever. Not only because of the magic it offered, but also because as soon as I returned to reality, despair would chime in with its usual song: "All is lost," he would say. "You will never go there again. There is no hope for you. Why not give up and walk with me. I will not tease you with springs of water and the smell of the breeze. I will keep you anchored in a reality where the lights of your dim cell and the cold metal bed frame remind you that you are fated for doom. This is your life, here with me. Your dreams and goals will only break your heart. I never will. I will promise you doom and gloom. You always know what to expect with me."

But the light would always faithfully step forward so that I could no longer see the shape of despair. The light would remind me, "All things are possible. Even that which is impossible is possible in the presence of the light. Your life is not over. It has only just begun. Let me show you the future. It is bright. It is warm. It welcomes your home."

> Life is not a spectator sport. If you're going to spend your whole life in the grandstand just watching what goes on, in my opinion, you're wasting your life.
>
> — JACKIE ROBINSON

CHAPTER 10

TIME BECOMES NEW

June 2014

All of my definitions had to change. I had to rework some, delete some, and add some. What I thought was love, wasn't love. What I thought was work, wasn't work. What I thought was faith, wasn't faith. It was time for a big overhaul. Even my definition of friendship was flawed and in need of a remodel.

When I thought back on the time I spent with people I believed were my friends, I was saddened. I placed myself in harm's way by surrounding myself with people who only cared for themselves. We spent countless hours at clubs and bars, talking and dancing the night away. But when the chips were down and I needed their love and support, they were nowhere to be found. Sure, they said all the right things. They said what I wanted to hear. But their words had no life because they were not backed up by any action. As a result, at the first sign of adversity, they scattered like ants in a rainstorm.

I spent my precious time with these people for years. I also spent my valuable money on them. They said words of reassurance that lured me into thinking that they were true friends. But once we were separated by jail walls, none of them came to visit. Their words of encouragement went silent, replaced with words of judgment. It made me wonder why I had spent so much time with them. There were moments with them that I had thought were real. But when they abandoned me in my hour of need — in my darkest days--I wondered if any of it had been genuine. Perhaps they could not be authentic. Maybe they hadn't had the benefit of going deep into the darkness to find the bottom of their souls.

When I reflected on the things that had been attractive to me, I realized that they were only the things of this world. I had been a slave to them. I believed in those things and trusted that life. But that life was built on a shaky foundation. I was at a junction — a crossroads. Those fake friends went one way, while I went to the other. It felt lonely. It felt isolating. But it was the path toward the truth. If I continued walking with them, I would be admitting that I did not care about the truth. It was here, at this critical point in my life, that truth radiated its light and the light reflected the truth. It was all about the truth. My court case would rely on the truth to free me. But even after that happened, the truth would have to be the vehicle in which I traveled down the path.

One day, as my days in jail dragged on, I suddenly had a new visitor. It was time. Time was not so easily shoved aside by the light. It stood shoulder to shoulder with the light. Time did not tease or taunt. But it also did not encourage or uplift. It was just always present. It was a constant reminder that I was losing precious moments. Every second had value to me. I realized then that I would take this principle with me everywhere I went for the rest of my life. I would never again waste time. I would treasure every minute as if it were my last.

There is a saying that if you give a person a fish, she or he will eat it for a day. If you teach a person to fish, she or he will eat for a lifetime. I did not want a handout. I certainly did not want anyone to do the work for me. I was willing, ready, and able to roll up my sleeves and get to work rebuilding my life. What I did need was a hand. Circumstances provide you with the opportunity to teach others about what you have been through and the lessons you have learned. (I will share some of those lessons in Part II of this book.)

The lesson is the reward. It is the payoff for all that you have been through to get where you are. Some people learn their lessons well. They are good students because they are open to hearing, learning, and receiving. Other students fight back against the teacher. They argue, debate, and resist the wisdom that is being shared with them, making them impossible to teach. So, the teacher ultimately gives up and walks away. As the lovely old bible verse says, "Do not throw your pearls before swine." No teacher wants to take their hard-earned wisdom and knowledge and share it with someone who pushes it away.

The same thing happens with lifeguards. If you have ever talked to a lifeguard, they will tell you how hard it is to save a drowning swimmer. Lifeguards have complained that their attempts to save the victim nearly cost them their life. Why? Because the drowning person's flailing about works against the efforts of the lifeguard to save them. And, sometimes, the drowning person will grab the lifeguard and pull them both underwater. Because of this, lifeguards approach the victim from behind so that they can get them to safety.

This principle applies to sharing knowledge and wisdom with others. I wanted to help people who seemed genuinely interested in receiving my assistance. However, you can only help those who want your help and are in a position to receive that help. Certain people are not available. They are arrogant, distant, unfocused, or disinterested.

In my situation I wanted help. I needed help. I made sure to put myself in a position where I could receive help. I put myself in the hands of those who could teach me. I learned to fish, and I was able to sustain myself through those dark days. The trial was ahead of me. There was no way I could get around it. I would have to face whatever was waiting for me inside that courtroom. I would have to prove myself to the legal justice system before I could prove myself to the world.

Thankfully, I put in the hard work before the trial. There were things I needed to learn to become the individual who could fight for his freedom. I had to shed so much of myself that was not useful in helping me achieve my goals. I had to learn new things: new skills, new belief systems, new attitudes, and new goals. I came into the jail as one man, but I would leave it a completely different man. I knew that I was a better man, no matter what the prosecutor was planning to say about me.

I had been to hell and back, and I had learned some things on the round trip. I had connected the dots. That is why the light is so important. The dots are impossible to connect in the darkness. The dots are dark, so in the darkness, you cannot see them. You need the light.

Sometimes, you have to go places that are far outside of your comfort zone. You have to embrace the discomfort like an old friend. Doing what you have always done and understood will only get you what you have always had. You have to do something different and new. You are reborn. You see with new eyes. You touch with new hands. You love with a new heart.

There were times I wanted to hide, I admit. I did not know when I would be free again, if ever. I was facing 32 years of life in prison. If convicted, I would have to serve at least 32 years. I was afraid of what it would mean to tell my story and bare my soul to the world. When you expose your soul, you expose your pain. You let people into the most private and secret parts of who you are. It is when you are the most vulnerable that you can be judged by others most harshly. I knew that I was taking a risk by deciding to share my story, but it was a risk I knew I had to take. It would be up to me to show that I was worthy of my freedom. I had learned to fish. Now I was fishing.

What guarantees can I make today? I know for sure that light is stronger than darkness. Yes, the darkness has a strong impact. But it is not able to extinguish the light. I know for sure that my life is what I decide it will be. If I fail to decide, the world will decide for me. It would put me in a box I do not want to be in.

The stories in the Bible are filled with lessons that apply to life. I started to read the Bible while I was in jail. I read about people who were incarcerated. They never lost their faith. They never gave up their hope. They always believed that some miracle would occur that would ultimately free them.

I read about Joseph.

He was born into a family that rejected him because he was special and gifted. They did not celebrate his worth. They threw him into a pit. This was his first jail. Then he was sold to slave traders, his second jail. Then he was sold to Potiphar to be his slave, his third jail.

Like me, Joseph was falsely accused and thrown into his fourth jail, a literal dungeon for criminals. His life went up and down like a roller coaster. He was unfairly judged by everyone, from his family to society at large. Even though he worked hard to prove himself, it seemed that his life kept getting worse and worse.

But he had worked hard to develop skills and he was connected to the light. That light shone on him when he was a very young boy and had remained with him throughout his life, even in his darkest places. Everything he set his hand to, he did well. He earned the respect and admiration of his owners as well as the prisoners with whom he was incarcerated. Despite the false accusation, he never let it change his perspective and outlook on life or faith. He did not wallow in his sorrows or see himself as a victim. He kept moving forward. He helped everyone he could, even in jail.

Then his moment came to shine. It was time for his next big move and he was ready. He stepped up when it counted and was able to win the trust of the Pharaoh, as well as save all of Egypt and many neighboring towns and villages. He was called the Prince of Egypt for his excellent work in staving off the effects of a famine. If it had not been for his genius plan to store grain during the seven years before the famine, millions would have died.

I read about Peter.

Peter's miraculous prison story began when he was arrested by King Herod, who hated Peter and his friends. Herod killed some and arrested others. He arrested Peter during Passover Week. It was a double slap in the face because this was a once-per-year Jewish holy day. It would be like arresting someone on Christmas Day, in our culture. King Herod was so crazed about making sure Peter did not escape, that he assigned extra soldiers to guard Peter. Peter was innocent, but King Herod's hatred was enough to seal his fate. At least, the King was willing to wait until after the Passover to have Peter judged, which would probably have ended in his death.

Peter was running out of time. His friends had gathered at a nearby house, praying day and night for his release. The night before he was to be judged and, likely, executed, the light came to him while he was asleep in his prison cell. The guards were still posted outside his door, with two more guards in the cell. They were chained to Peter—one on his left and one on his right—so that his escape was impossible.

Suddenly, a blinding light shone in the prison (I believe it was the same light I saw when I was in prison). The light-filled every dark place. It was so strong! The chains fell from Peter's wrists. An angel woke Peter and told him to put on his coat and shoes. Peter was in a daze. I can understand precisely how he felt. I, too, was in a daze when the light came to me. Peter believed for a moment that it was all a beautiful and fantastic dream. But it was real. It was true. He walked behind the angel as they headed toward the door. They walked right by the soldiers who were in a trance. Peter found himself standing on the streets of the city.

I read about Jesus.

Of course, there is the prison story of Jesus. As hard as the officials of the two governments tried, they could not find any crime that they could make stick. But they continued to accuse him. While in prison, he was beaten and ridiculed. Finally, the leader of the government decided to let the people decide if Jesus should die. They condemned him even though he had only done good. Jesus was beaten again, given a crown made of prickly thorns, and forced to carry his cross from the jail to the place of his execution. He died a ghastly death with his ripped flesh on display for all to see. Then he was sealed in a tomb in the hopes that everyone would forget about him. But the light broke forth and Jesus came out of the darkness to declare himself the light of the world.

We can be a light in the world regardless of who we are and where we have come from. There is so much that each of us can give if we press into purpose.

Story after story reminds us that the presence of the light pushes away the darkness, even in jail. I can share how I feel today because I am living in that light. Some people stay in the darkness. It is more comfortable for them. It is the place where they can hide. They do not have to work hard in the dark place. They can retreat. The light exposes everything, and that is uncomfortable for some.

Over the years, I think back to the dark times. I have learned to stay away from the darkness. You haven't learned anything if you don't use what you learn. You simply struggle day after day. If someone shares their knowledge with you, but you refuse to put their wisdom into action, your life will never change.

Life is all about managing: managing your emotions, managing your gifts, managing your blessings, managing your relationships, managing your money. Whatever you abuse, you lose. And whatever you neglect or ignore will fade away and die from lack of nourishment. I knew people who were making a six-figure income who never had any money. They were always begging, borrowing, and stealing their way to the top. But they couldn't stay at the top because they did not manage what they had. They had no goals or systems to preserve their blessings. So they lost them and had to continually start over again to acquire what they wanted and needed.

We must learn from our situations. Nothing should be wasted. The world can be cold. People call the world "dog eat dog." But that thinking is based on fear and paranoia. You can't be productive if you are walking around fearful of who is out to destroy you. It is far better to put the mind in a positive vibration. Always hope. Always believe. Always think those good things will happen.

I am grateful that I made it through the storm.

I am grateful that the light found me.

I am grateful that the darkness is gone.

I am grateful that my path is clear.

I am grateful that nothing else is hidden.

Today, I set my mind on what I want to achieve. I had set my mind on freeing myself from jail and I did. I proved my innocence and escaped that life sentence. In the process, I received a new life. Nothing is impossible now.

PART 2

The Lessons

I learned that courage was not the absence of fear, but the triumph over it. The brave man is not he who does not feel afraid, but he who conquers that fear… Everyone can rise above their circumstances and achieve success if they are dedicated to, and passionate about what they do… It always seems impossible until it's done… Do not judge me by my successes, judge me by how many times I fell and got back up again… It is in the character of growth that we should learn from both pleasant and unpleasant experiences.

— NELSON MANDELA

INTRODUCTION TO THE LESSONS

In a world fixated on living a long life, living the good life, and obtaining a better quality of life, it is easy to overlook the importance of the life to come. Take the time to look beyond the things of this world and consider your eternity. This will help you to keep perspective when you are faced with adversity.

Part II of this book illustrates the gifts and gems that can be found in adversity. I share with you how I survived the darkest time of my life and how I reshaped my destiny. Here are the lessons that adversity taught me.

ADVERSITY ILLUMINATES PRIORITIES

A great man knows when to set aside the important things to accomplish the vital ones.
— Brandon Sanderson

As I mentioned, I would not allow anything I had been through to be wasted. I would use it all. I would not allow those dark days of jail to be all that I remembered. But I wanted to know that I had grown from what I experienced.

One of the first lessons I learned was that I needed to set priorities in my life. Adversity helps you to put things in their proper perspective. As author Steven R. Covey wrote, *"Most of us spend too much time on what is urgent and not enough time on what is important."* The task of prioritizing is an important but difficult one. It is amazing to think about the fact that there are pressures we face in this age that no other human has had to manage. In just the past 100 years, the world has changed completely. There were 75% fewer people 100 years ago. It was rare to see or hear about a car accident. The majority of women were full-time parents in the home, and without a paying job. Most homes did not have television, precious few had telephones, and none had computers. Half of the people enjoyed the luxury of radio and those who did not, enjoyed an open invitation to stop by and listen at a friend's house. A major illness almost always meant death. The average life expectancy was less than 50 in 1900. There were no planes in the sky until 1903. More than half of the population lived in rural areas. Finally, a household had an average of 5 people, more than today.

Time spent engaged in purely recreational activities has dropped significantly from those glory days of a hundred years ago. In developed countries like the U.S., the decline is stark and alarming. Nearly half of Americans reported that they participated in no outdoor recreational activities last year. None! Any child of the 60s and 70s will regale you with stories about how the streets were filled with children after school playing jump rope, hopscotch, baseball, and basketball. Children walking, running, and riding bikes were a common sight. But in communities across America, and other western countries, time spent having fun away from technology is surprisingly low. More than 80% of Americans say that they do not spend time outdoors even once per week. As Lisa Aangeenbrug, Executive Director of the Outdoor Foundation, says,

> *It's been going on since the early 2000s. We saw the largest single-year drop-off in 2007, and it's just not gotten any better since then. It might go up slightly, then it goes down, it goes up slightly and it goes down. It's a pretty stagnant number.*

According to a recent study, in the past year:

- Only 18% of people took at least one walk, jog, or run.
- Only 16% of people went fishing.
- Only 15% of people rode bikes.
- Only 14% of people went on a hike.
- Only 14% of people went camping or backpacking.

Activities that simply delight the eyes and feed the soul, such as visiting a zoo or museum, playing an instrument, reading a book, tossing the ball with our children, or going to a play, are plummeting at a rapid rate. Only 9% of us played a board game last week. Even taking vacations is declining as a part of American and Western culture. Almost 50% of American workers surrendered their paid vacation to work, and as many as 10% reported that they do not take vacations for fear of falling behind.

With the advent of mind-blowing technology and innovation comes a set of issues that are challenging, to say the least. New technology is expensive. It can be time-consuming to learn and implement. But the biggest issue is that life can be chaotic, fast-paced, and rushed. Having more to do, unfortunately, does not come with the benefit of having more time in which to do it. The same 24 hours we have always had must now be applied to, in some cases, an exponentially greater number of tasks. That can be challenging even for the most talented, organized, and intelligent among us. It is hard to find peace when you are being pulled in 1000 directions. And it is harder to focus on the things that matter — the things that will move you closer to your dreams.

Futurists and proponents of the theory of singularity argue that human beings are already machines because of our dependence on smartphones. We have a piece of machinery that is, basically, always attached to the end of our arm. We don't allow ourselves to be without it for any length of time. Our attachment to and dependence on electronics have made us android-style robots, to some extent. Addiction to smartphone use is considered quite normal in a global society. Even in countries considered "third world" and economically disadvantaged, the one luxury many people will afford is a cellular or smartphone. If you do not believe that the majority of people are inches away from becoming an android, consider these statistics:

- 80% of people take their phones to bed with them.
- 85% of people find it socially acceptable to use their phones in the bathroom.
- 90% of people experience physical symptoms if they lose or break their phones.

An MIT study had college students give up their smartphones for one day. The majority of students reported severe reactions like anxiety, depression, and confusion. They also showed higher blood pressure and heart rates while they were without their smartphones.

The Radiological Conference of North America found that there were visible and measurable changes in the brain including brain chemistry and physical structure because of smartphone addiction.

Smartphone addiction is real and prevalent. Psychologists have added it to the Diagnostic and Statistical Manual of Mental Disorders. But what is going on with our smartphones? Do most people spend their time on their smartphones? Are they buying stocks, researching for a paper, or reading books? No! The average American is spending about 6 hours on their phones daily. Social media seems to have consumed the majority of our screen time, and the majority of that social media time is entertaining rather than productive. Here is the breakdown of how that time is spent:

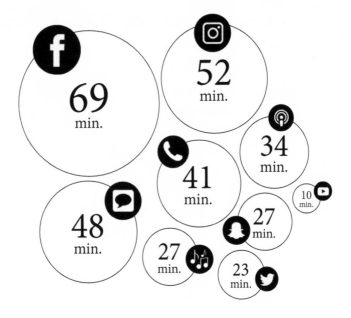

It is not only smartphones that are stealing our time and complicating our lives. Our cars are essentially computerized now and require additional time and focus to operate, even though the changes were designed to make life easier. Television sets are also highly computerized and can connect to the internet and other users around the world. We've even managed to make something as simple as a doorbell into a major technological event, with video doorbells that allow us to see who is visiting when we are not home.

It is not over. It is growing. The future of technology is vast. Self-driving cars are expected to be rolled out in a big way over the next couple of years. Brain wave passwords will make remembering your password nothing more than a memory. Tactile, virtual-reality makers create gaming experiences where players can reach out and touch their avatars. Floating farms envision a time when we can use the air above to grow our food. Clothing that monitors your physical health is currently being tested. And even flying cars are not that far away. But will all of this technology make life simpler or more complicated?

All this innovation has clear advantages. However, it would be foolhardy to ignore the time and effort it takes to install and operate all of these devices. The biggest drain is the money it all costs, which causes us to work longer and harder so that we can have the latest gadget. Since we all love our current jobs so much, there should be no problem with working more, right? Wrong!

The time we spend at work represents a significant part of our lives. Since it can be argued, at least statistically, that smartphone use (the way it is done by most users) is not the most productive way to spend our time on earth, perhaps we should turn to work to find meaning. Sadly, the statistics there are equally as alarming. Most adults who work a typical American workweek spend at least a quarter of their lives at work. People who are prone to work overtime and weekends spend considerably more. So, since a fourth of our lives is spent at work, one would assume that most of us enjoy the time we spend there. The truth is quite the opposite.

Employee engagement in work is slipping year by year. According to a Gallup poll, 70% of employees reported feeling disengaged from their work. A comprehensive Harvard Business Review study reports that people trust a perfect stranger more than they trust their bosses. Almost 53% of American workers state that they hate their jobs. Finally, a Global Studies report showed that 79% of people who quit their jobs did so not because they did not feel they were being paid enough, but because they were unhappy at work and felt unappreciated.

We seem to have complicated the employment landscape so much that we have made ourselves miserable. Anecdotally speaking, how many people do you know who are happy at their jobs? The numbers speak volumes about the general discontent with our use of time at work. So that must mean that we are spending plenty of time having fun, decompressing from our high-pressure work, and de-stressing to cope with life more efficiently. Wrong again!

Adversity can help us. It can help us to slow down and focus on what matters most in our lives. As G. Michael Hopf said in *Those Who Remain*,

Hard times create strong men.
Strong men create good times.
Good times create weak men.
And, weak men create hard times.

What can save us from this addiction to technology, mindless attraction to entertainment, and the feeling of being stuck in jobs where we do not make a difference? Adversity. It may sound strange or even insensitive to suggest that adversity can be a positive thing. But the truth is often shocking. And the truth is that adversity helps us. Adversity helps to reveal what is important in life and sets us on the right course when we have gotten off track. We are wasting time. No one wants to say it because no one wants to hear it. But that does not negate the veracity of the argument that people are majoring in minor activities and minoring in major activities.

On September 10, Linda Randazzo went to bed. She had an early day ahead, as she did most days. She got up, went to work, and set about her usual routine. Within 30 minutes, her desk began to shake and moved away from the wall. The year was 2001, and her building had just been struck by an airplane. She ran for the narrow staircase trying to escape. Linda began to pray as she descended the stairs. As she said, "I was leaning on my faith as hard as I could lean." Her legs were going numb partially from fear and from the 35 flights she had to descend to escape. Her back had begun to seize and the pain was crippling. She could no longer walk but remaining in the stairwell meant certain death.

She prayed fervently, "Lord, I can't go on. Can you send an angel to walk with me?" She said at that moment a feeling of peace washed over her. She felt a firm hand on the small of her back, the pain disappeared, and the numbness was gone. The hand continued to push her down the stairs. When she reached the landing, a firefighter told her to run for the door. She remembers the moment when she saw sunlight again. Once she was out of the building, she and hundreds of others were led away from the site just as the building collapsed behind them. That day, Linda Randazzo says, her faith was strengthened. She had always believed, but her certainty in God's providence and the presence of angels to protect her was solidified. She realized that the only thing that had mattered to her before was work, work, work. But when the walls began to shake, life itself, her family, and the joys of her world took on new meaning.

Chasing money and power has its place. But it can never replace the joy of snuggling with your loved ones while you watch a funny movie or take a stroll arm in arm to watch the sunset.

ADVERSITY TEACHES PERSEVERANCE

The most beautiful people we have known are those who have known defeat, known suffering, known struggle, known loss, and have found their way out of the depths. . . Beautiful people do not just happen.

— Elisabeth Kübler-Ross

In Hell's Kitchen, in their burgeoning Manhattan neighborhood, Jackie and Frank were anxiously awaiting the birth of their first son. The day finally came when Jackie went into labor. It was meant to be a joyous day. But something was not right. The pains she was feeling indicated something had gone awry and her baby was in trouble. Frank rushed her to the hospital, but the situation had already become critical. Doctors worked to save the baby's life by using forceps to help with the birth. But an unfortunate slip of the doctor's hand struck the baby in the head, severed a nerve, and caused facial paralysis. His lip, tongue, and chin would sag forever. His facial expression would be in a permanent snarl and his speech would be slurred.

Fast forward thirty years to Hollywood, California. The Academy Awards. The year is 1977 and the room is tense. Epic movies like *All the President's Men* and *Bound for Glory* are nominated for the Academy's top prize. But the award goes to a low-budget sleeper starring a virtually unknown actor. That little boy, with the lazy lip and the speech impediment, was Sylvester Stallone.

In an interview about his adversities, Stallone remarked that just before being cast in *Rocky*, he had tried to sell his dog because he did not have enough money to feed him. Stallone was down to his last $106.00.

> *And then one night, I went out to see Muhammad Ali fight Chuck Wepner. And what I saw was pretty extraordinary. I saw a man called 'The Bayonne Bleeder' fight the greatest fighter who ever lived. And for one brief moment, this supposed stumblebum turned out to be magnificent. And he lasted and knocked the champ down. I wondered if this isn't a metaphor for life.*

Stallone did not just star in *Rocky*, he wrote it. He used the pain and trauma of his childhood as a catalyst to fuel his writing. It was clear to him that people would embrace the story of a man who had been through tough times and overcame them to go the distance and win the title of Champ. It only took him ninety days to bang out a script. The Hollywood producers loved the script. But, Sylvester Stallone in the lead? Not so much. His facial abnormalities and signature slur were a concern. They did not think America would gravitate to such deficiencies. They wanted to try Burt Reynolds or Ryan O'Neil instead.

This almost seems humorous today, since those facial features are part of what we love about Stallone. Our admiration for this unique and great actor is huge. Could you imagine anyone else in the role of Rocky? People came by the millions to see the movie, which was the highest-grossing film of 1976. It cost just $1 million to make and raked in more than $275 million in revenue. The movie received an impressive nine Oscar nominations and won three of them.

It was Sylvester Stallone's adversities that made him so perfect in portraying Rocky. He depicted the sheer will and determination of the archetypal underdog who rises far above his adversities to achieve the highest prize. Stallone was paid just $360,000 for the script. But it was not the money he was after. He knew that it was his destiny to play that role. All of the trauma he had suffered in his life seemed to prepare him for this specific role. It was his purpose that drove him. Stallone is an iconic figure who has reprised this role in several of the sequels, including the latest iteration, *Creed*, for which he received a Best Actor nomination, a Golden Globe, and an NAACP Image Award win.

Life is all about our destiny. It comes down to some basic questions: Why are we here? What are we meant to do and be in the world? Discovering our destiny is no easy feat, particularly in the modern age. Perhaps years ago, when the world was slower, it might have been easier to know one's purpose in the world. But the world moves at an alarming pace today, and it is enough to make one's head spin.

Destiny speaks to a person's passion, drive, interest, and (more importantly) calling. If you believe that people have a calling, then you must also accept that the purpose of life is to uncover that calling and then figure out how to walk in it. Some believe that the question of destiny is the most important question they will answer because finding it gives their lives direction. Each step they take toward fulfilling that destiny gives them peace and floods them with immeasurable joy.

The problem is that life is often like a rocket ship. It takes off and moves so quickly that course corrections become quite difficult. When a spaceship veers off of its vectors, it must employ thrusters that yank it out of the clutches of gravitational pull and set it on a new path. Even the smallest mistake in navigation can cost thousands of miles, lots of fuel, and quite a bit of time to correct. The same is true for large ships. The time and energy it takes to turn a large ship is massive. Such is the case with anything big like a corporation or a country. Big things are tough to course correct.

The same is true for your big life. If you have not found your destiny, you are off course. Your experiences may be critical clues to your ultimate destiny. However, you will need massive amounts of time and energy to get back on course. That is the function of adversity. It sets you on the path to be and do the things you were uniquely formed to be and do. If Stallone had not been living from job to job, he could not have taken advantage of the opportunity to use a free ticket to see a fight that changed his life. Looking even further back, if he had not been born with his unique disability, he may not have been able to portray such a compelling character facing adversity, as Rocky Balboa.

It is interesting to think about what your life might have been like without adversity. Without it, you would not be the person you are today. You would not desire what you desire. In fact, for most people who claim to have discovered their destiny, they point directly to their adversities as the driving force that brought them to their fate. Rather than grappling with the adversity and trauma of your past, it may be more beneficial to take a step back and ask yourself what they have been trying to tell you. It may very well be that your destiny requires certain skills, attitudes, determination, or fortitude that you do not already possess but will need to be the person you are destined to become. More often than not, there may be character flaws within you that will not accommodate where you are going. You must shed them if you are going to walk into a new place in your life.

Is it worth it to push through adversity to discover your destiny? Absolutely! The message is to persevere. Even in the darkest night, the faintest light shines brightly. People who have discovered their destiny enjoy amazing benefits.

ADVERSITY UNCOVERS PURPOSE

The greatest thing in this world is not so much where we stand as in what direction we are moving.
— **Johann wolfgang von Goethe**

.

All kinds of unhealthy results of living outside your purpose can show up in your life. There are physical manifestations. According to doctors at Psychology Today Magazine, living without purpose can be bad for your health — literally. People who seek psychological help with the complaint of feeling lost and purposeless often report physical ailments such as headaches, upset stomach, soreness, and chronic pain. This feeling that the body is unwell is often called dis-ease, which eventually can lead to an untreatable, chronic condition. No amount of medication or other therapies show any demonstrable or long-term effect, because the source of the pain stems from the sense in a person that his or her life is off-course.

There are also emotional manifestations of not living your purpose. Some people visit psychologists and doctors complaining of a frequent shuddering sensation. Psychologist, Dr. Sam Louie of the University of California Davis, calls this "soul revolt." It is the inner being rising and seeking to shake the body into action toward the thing the soul craves that the mind has not yet discovered. These symptoms often subside with a career change, spiritual intentionality, or other life-altering activities.

There are also environmental manifestations. Loss of purpose is usually depicted in the state of your surroundings. Are you surrounded by things that bring you joy and peace? Does your environment speak to who you want to be or is it a sobering reminder of who you have been? Dr. Louis cites behaviors like excessive drinking, recreational drugs use, or binge-watching of TV and movies as signs that life has gotten off its trajectory and requires a course correction to bring healing and wholeness to mind, body, soul, and spirit.

Victor Frankl was born in Austria in 1905. While he was still a very young boy, the Nazis came to his home and took Victor, along with his pregnant mother, his father, and his brother, and placed them in a concentration camp in Auschwitz. They lived under the cruel rule of the Nazis until the decision was made to exterminate the people in the camps. His entire family was killed in a single day. Frankl escaped and wrote about his experiences. As a result of his adversities and his ultimate search for his destiny, he developed a school of psychology called logotherapy. He has written dozens of books, including the bestseller, *Man's Search for Meaning*, in which he says:

> *What man needs is not a tensionless state*
> *but rather the striving and struggling*
> *for some goal worthy of him.*
> *What he needs is not the discharge*
> *of tension at any cost,*
> *but the call of a potential meaning*
> *waiting to be fulfilled by him.*

It is tempting to want to escape adversity. Let's face it: it's painful, it's uncertain, and it always seems to last too long. But out of adversity can come the great gift of discovery — the discovery of one's true purpose in being. There are far too many benefits to name, but here is just a small sampling of why it matters to know your own WHY:

Living your destiny makes life fun.

No matter if your destiny is to serve truckers at a country road rest stop or to discover the cure for a deadly virus, when you are living in destiny, you are full of bliss. Look at people who work long hours playing basketball or building houses. Look at people with seemingly difficult jobs, such as working in Intensive Care with critically ill patients or performing death-defying stunts in a motion picture. They love what they do. Days are not merely the laborious quest for a paycheck. Instead, it is the fulfillment of destiny. As the famous quote goes, "If you do what you love, you'll never work a day in your life."

Living your destiny fosters integrity.

This is a tough concept to grasp. Once you do, however, it will cause a paradigm shift that registers on the Richter scale. People who are out of sync with their destiny are involved in activities that are not the truest expressions of themselves. They are living a subpar reality that does not capitalize on the best of who they are. When you live in the place of destiny, there is a truth that comes from the core of you. Others can see, feel, hear, and trust this. People who do not know who they are or why they are here come across as fake or incomplete. But people living in alignment with their destiny know what they are about. They live in alignment with their soul and their purpose. They are not trying to be something they are not. That is where I was living. I was doing work that was not the highest expression of myself. I was not pursuing all of the things my soul craved because I had not taken the time to learn what my heart and soul wanted.

Living your destiny promotes focus and passion.

There are too many people in the world who are living lives that lack direction. They hate their jobs. They feel trapped in their own lives. They have no time for outside interests. It is a sad existence. Worst of all, they do not possess the fire in their belly that rockets them out of the bed in the morning and sends them flying toward activities that bring them excitement. Purpose brings passion. You will not be easily sidetracked into doing things that do not feed your soul when you are living intentionally in the world. You have a certain clarity that others cannot enjoy. You know exactly what to say yes to and what to say no to because you can measure each request against your purpose.

People who live on purpose do not waste time because their minutes, hours, days, weeks, and years are booked with activities they know they are meant to do. Any other projects are distractions they can reject with confidence. There is no substitute for living on purpose. You have boundless energy. You are excited to do it. Even when it is hard, you keep going because you are thrilled to be in the right place at the right time doing the right thing.

Living your destiny makes you good at what you do.

You have felt this effect if you have ever been served by someone who is living outside of their destiny. They are dull, lethargic, disinterested, and unmotivated. They do not serve you with a smile. They feel that your presence represents an unwelcome intrusion.

This is not so with people who live in and on purpose. Your presence simply gives them another opportunity to do the thing they love to do. So, they perform with excellence. Because they perform with excellence, they get better and better at what they do, no matter how complicated or menial the task is. They attract people because destiny is alluring. They will give more than what is requested or expected because their acts of service feed them rather than deplete them. Their sense of value is wrapped up in bringing value to others. They are fired up when they get to do the things they love. They are filled up by pouring out. It is the great paradox of a powerful life that is lived amidst the throes of destiny. That is why you often see actors, athletes, doctors, scientists, and others at their craft long into the night. They are so enthralled and engaged, it never feels like work. They want to spend their lives on purpose.

To be clear, your destiny is not the one that was chosen for you by your parents. It may not even be the one that seems obvious to the people who know you. ("You have a pretty voice: you should be a singer." Or, "You are tall, so you should be a basketball player.") All of those attempts to shape destiny are likely to fall flat. Destiny is not always obvious. People remark that they "stumble" into it. What they mean is that adversity (usually suffered from pursuing false destiny) moved them toward the thing that they were born to do.

In a gripping article in the Huffington Post, blogger Cate Pane outlines the tragedy of missed destiny and the glorious redemption that comes from learning one's purpose:

A tall, brown-haired 20-something stood up in the middle of the crowded audience and reluctantly approached the microphone. She began to chronicle the seemingly never-ending hours spent studying and interning and working in residency. It had been a long and arduous process to become a physician.

Then, she was asked the million-dollar question: "What made you decide to become a doctor?" She hesitated. She looked perplexed. Slowly, a look of clarity filled her eyes as she gathered up the gumption to utter in a voice choking back the tears: "I guess it was what my parents always dreamed for me. I never questioned it. I was great at math and science. I aced the MCATs."

As she grew up, medical school was part of the destiny on her bright and promising horizon. "But," she acknowledged, "I guess I never really wanted to become a doctor. I hate it. I'd like to do something else!"

The audience erupted in joyous applause as this lovely young woman had reached an epiphany. The camera moved to the triumphant talk show host. Her daytime program spotlighting career passion had helped this full-fledged physician to ditch her scrubs and figure out what she wanted to do with her life. For some reason, that episode and that miserable, young doctor have remained in my head for years. It is an idea that I just can't shake. How could a parent possibly guide a child into a career they never had a passion for in the first place?

It is never too late to reinvent yourself. History offers us tale after tale of people who learned their place in the world through their adversities. Bible stories are replete with examples of people who had missed destiny but found it again through adversity. Moses's life began with adversity. He was floated down a river to spare him the death of all newborns being executed by the Pharaoh's army. He ended up in Pharaoh's home. But he went on the run from the law after saving the life of an Egyptian slave by killing one of the Pharaoh's soldiers. He spent years in the desert suffering. But he learned from what he suffered and returned, ultimately saving the lives of millions of slaves.

Joseph was despised by his brothers and they threw him into a pit, where they left him for dead. He was sold into slavery and ended up in the Pharaoh's prison. As a result, he met a prisoner who would recommend him to the Pharaoh as an interpreter of dreams when the Pharaoh was being tormented by dreams. Joseph was summoned from the dungeon to interpret the dream. His interpretation and subsequent advice saved the lives of millions of people.

So the reward of purpose makes the pain of adversity a worthwhile endeavor. It is much like mining for diamonds. The quest for diamonds can be filled with adversity, which partly accounts for their value. Diamond mines are often 1500 feet deep. Once the difficult task of mining for diamonds is complete and the precious stones are unearthed, the work is just beginning. The stones must still be cut and polished.

I believe your quest toward destiny will be just as rigorous. You will need to dig deep. You will have to unearth all that is powerful, unique, and unmistakably inherent to your being because that is where destiny lies. It is very rarely lying on the surface. It is almost always lying deep beneath. That is why adversity is required to jackhammer your purpose out of the mud and rock of your soul, polish it, and make it glimmer.

People who have completed this process will cheer you on to victory because they know the great treasures that lie on the other side of adversity. Those treasures are not merely for your enjoyment. They are gifts to the world no matter how big your world is. If you have found yourself growing complacent and are stuck in your present reality, we will talk about how to shake yourself out of that place in the next chapter. For now, let's look at one more hero whose willingness to ensure adversity resulted in great benefits for the whole world.

Jean Dominique-Bauby was a journalist living in France in the 20th-century. He was faithfully following his chosen path as a journalist and had joined the staff of the famed Elle magazine. However, he suffered a massive stroke at the age of 43, leaving him in a coma for weeks. Unable to speak or move, he could only learn a system of blinking to communicate with those around him. From this paralyzed place, he decided that it was his destiny to write a book. Using his blinking method, he communicated to a scribe who wrote out the words to The Diving Bell and the Butterfly. The book became an instant bestseller across Europe selling millions of copies. It took more than 200,000 blinks to write it, and more than two minutes to write each word. Adversity helped him find his purpose, and his perseverance allowed him to give the gift of his book to the world.

The memory of that event has only just come back to me, now doubly painful: regret for a vanished past and, above all, remorse for lost opportunities . . . unable to love, the chances we failed to seize, the moments of happiness we allowed to drift away. Today it seems to me that my whole life was nothing but a string of those small near misses: a race whose result we know beforehand but in which we fail to bet on the winner . . . Does it take the harsh light of disaster to show a person's true potential?"

I think it does take the "harsh light of disaster" to show you who you were meant to be. It takes the cruel winds of trouble to blow you toward your destiny. It takes the blinding rain of trauma to wash away the grime that builds upon the soul. And once you have been sandblasted by adversity, you find yourself shiny, polished, and fit to have a powerful impact on your world.

ADVERSITY CLEARS OUT COMPLACENCY

Adversity is like a strong wind. I don't mean just that it holds us back from places we might otherwise go. It also tears away from us all but the things that cannot be torn, so that afterward we see ourselves as we are, and not merely as we might like to be.

— Arthur Golden

I have to admit, I had it good before adversity struck. I was living large. I was surrounded by beautiful women. I was wheeling and dealing. Life was everything I thought I wanted it to be. But I had not truly challenged myself.

Before we talk about what complacency IS, let's spend a moment exploring what it is NOT. Complacency is not contentment. Contentment is a positive attribute and something you should always seek. Contentment is a place of extreme gratitude for the blessings of life. The drive to acquire more material possessions, awards, and achievements means that the focus of life has shifted outward rather than inward. A person dissatisfied with their current situation lacks contentment. When we see that life is not measured in dollars and cents or measured by our possessions, we can find contentment. Besides, we in the Western world are wealthy by any reasonable measurement.

According to an article in Business Insider Magazine, even the very rich do not see themselves as rich. The article has a shocking title: "Only 13% of Millionaires Think They're Rich." Ameriprise Financial studied 3,000 Americans who had assets totaling at least one million dollars. Here is what they found:

- 25% of them considered themselves middle class
- 60% referred to themselves as upper-middle class
- 3% called themselves poor

The interesting thing about the study is that to participate, respondents had to have assets worth at least $1,000,000. But many of them felt they needed more before they would be rich. People who were surveyed in

San Francisco, for example, claim that it would take at least $4,000,000 before they would be wealthy.

But most people in the world live on far less in a week than we in the United States spend on a typical trip to Starbucks or McDonald's. Learning to be content is a powerful affirmation of all the good that has already happened in your life.

The global pandemic and the Coronavirus (COVID-19) ravaged communities around the world, killing millions and infecting millions more. If you are alive to read this book, you are fortunate. But you probably know some people who did not survive 2020. Plenty of people in the United States and around the world lost their jobs. In the United States, 20,000,000 people filed unemployment claims due to the pandemic. So, if you are reading this and you have a job, you are blessed.

In countries that were already ravaged by poverty, COVID-19 had much less effect on contentment. One African man said that the people in his village felt no economic impact because they have always lived simply. Their homes and cars are not threatened, as they live in houses they built themselves. They did not have to worry about a missed mortgage payment and someone coming to repossess their car. The people of his village rode animals, walked, or rode bikes to get to the places they needed to go. They had no car payments, insurance, or costly maintenance. They grew their food and raised their own livestock, so their food supply was not interrupted. So, for them, the impact has not been economic, but rather emotional due to the loss of life. They are free to grieve the loss of people they love because they are not simultaneously consumed with worry over money.

Contentment is a powerful tool in your arsenal for many reasons. Contentment allows you to bear adversity without adding needless pressures. Let me explain. The great poet Henry Wadsworth Longfellow wrote, "Into each life, some rain must fall." He was right. Every person, from princes to paupers, experiences adversity. It cannot be avoided by any living thing, whether it be plants, animals, or humans.

However, in addition to the adversity that life naturally brings, there are adversities we heap upon ourselves unnecessarily. Many people add to the adversity they experience by overextending their credit and going deeply into debt. The slightest wind could knock them over.

We must learn to be content even amid our adversity. It is not realistic to think that we should never experience adversity, never be disappointed, or never suffer loss. One Indian tribe has a saying:

ALL SUNSHINE MAKES A DESERT.

Be honest. A life filled with only sunshine and roses would have absolutely no meaning. Without rain, no amount of sunshine could make flowers grow. Tough times are a part of life, but they are a necessary part of life. Adversity forces us out of our comfortable places, where everything is familiar and understood.

While contentment is great, complacency is not. The proverbial comfort zone really can become a very dangerous place to live. Yet, millions of people land there and get stuck, like feet in quicksand. It is wise to leave your comfort zone. It is where all growth happens. If you do not stretch and challenge yourself, life can quickly pass you by. Before you know it, life has happened and you could be left with regret. Yewande jinadu, Founder of CareerLife Nigeria, has this to say about comfort,

> *Comfort is overrated. Keeping things the way they have been is not good for our careers. Even when we think we are having a nice career (good pay, proximity to home, interesting job description), we need to get uncomfortable to succeed. Ask the Generation X and the Baby Boomers (age 39-72) who have gotten to the plateau of their career, they will have interesting things to tell you. This is not to bring about discontentment or cause any type of confusion. However, being too comfortable has its negative impact on growth. To avoid this kind of mistake in the future . . . [you] should beware and act deliberately.*

Why bother stepping out of your comfort zone? It is a path to peace, and that peace can only be acquired by knowing you have spent your life in the best way possible.

Your comfort zone may feel perfectly fine to your physical being. The days are all the same. You know exactly what to expect. You get up at the same time. You go to bed at the same time. You have the same cup of coffee each day. You eat the same cycle of meals. And on and on the sameness and familiarity goes. But your brain is inwardly screaming that it wants out of this mindless existence. It wants a challenge. It needs to be pushed and stretched for it to stay viable and healthy. It grows increasingly restless when it has no new problem to work out.

The days are long, but the years are short. Ask anyone over the age of 40. They will tell you that they were 18 once and they blinked — and suddenly they are 40. It doesn't take long for life to roll on by. Beware of complacency and move outside of your comfort zone!

ADVERSITY TRAINS THE SOUL

Step up or step aside.

— **Christopher Titus**

We often think that doing the safe thing is the best idea. But, actually, it is quite risky. The safe thing is appealing to us because it mitigates the possibility of failure and, consequently, adversity. But fear of failure and adversity is an expensive proposition as *Self-Renewal* author, John Gardner writes in his book:

> *We pay a heavy price for our fear of failure. It is a powerful obstacle to growth. It assures the progressive narrowing of the personality and prevents exploration*

and experimentation. There is no learning without some difficulty and fumbling. If you want to keep on learning, you must keep on risking failure — all your life. It's as simple as that.

Creators, innovators, and earth-shakers try and fail often. That is what makes them successful and impactful. It is not because they are smarter, better connected, or more driven. It is because they are constantly forcing their brains to imagine new possibilities in spite of the fear. It might seem odd to refer to growing, stretching, reaching, and trying new things as a path to peace, since it involves a lot of research, hard work, and tenacity to overcome obstacles. Yet, this is precisely what our brains require to continue heightening and sharpening their function. This is particularly true for people as they age. It is a tragedy that the wisest and most experienced among us (the elders in society) shrink into the background when they have so much to give and share.

Furthermore, the secret to staying young is both physical fitness and neural stimulation. Doctors at Harvard Health have found that pushing the brain to work harder as you age is the primary factor in determining longevity in mental acuity. They refer to it as "mental gymnastics." Activities like completing puzzles, math problems, drawing, painting, and building are all effective at keeping the mind sharp.

Another way to challenge the brain, though, is to pursue the vision. The simple act of working through the challenges and adversities that come from chasing your vision is enough to stimulate your mind.

There is a spiritual aspect to this venture as well. The human spirit is indomitable. It is resilient. Adversity is spiritual training and can lead to the best parts of life. Roy T. Bennett in *The Light in the Heart*, says

Your hardest times often lead to
the greatest moments of your life.
Keep going. Tough situations
build strong people in the end.

One of the greatest presidents to ever serve the highest office in the land was Abraham Lincoln. He is also an amazing example of how adversity trains our soul for great things. We all know the stories of his great accomplishments and have heard his fascinating story. But, as always, there is a story behind the story and it includes much adversity. The history books tell us about his humble start in life. He was born to Thomas and Nancy Lincoln in a one-room log cabin in rural Hardin County, Kentucky. When he became a man, he took two jobs. He worked as a shopkeeper for part of the day and was also the local postmaster.

Lincoln faced challenges many of us can hardly imagine. He was not able to just attend school like children do today. The school day was just three hours for Lincoln because he had to leave class to work on the family farm. He worked on a riverboat that moved cargo up and down the Mississippi River, from Illinois to Louisiana. Unable to afford quality legal education, Abraham Lincoln satisfied his thirst to learn the law by teaching himself. He spent every waking moment poring over legal books and briefs until he felt he was ready to take the bar exam. He took it and passed it on the first try.

Abraham Lincoln married the love of his life, Mary. The couple had four children. But during their parenting years, adversity struck. Their son William contracted typhoid fever and died at the age of twelve. As he sat by the boy's deathbed waiting for him to breathe his last, Lincoln said, "My poor boy. He was too good for this earth. God has called him home. I know that he is much better off in heaven, but we loved him so much. It is hard, hard to have him die!"

The third of the Lincoln children, Edward, also suffered greatly. He never made it to his fourth year before cancer ravaged his young body and devastated Abraham Lincoln beyond words. In his grief and pain, it was rumored that he wrote a poem and sent it to the newspapers anonymously. It expresses the heart-rending agony of a parent whose young son has just died:

> *Those midnight stars are sadly dimmed,*
> *That late so brilliantly shone,*
> *And the crimson tinge from cheek and lip,*
> *With the heart's warm life has flown—*
> *The angel of death was hovering nigh,*
> *And the lovely boy was called to die.*
> *The silken waves of his glossy hair*
> *Lie still over his marble brow,*
> *And the pallid lip and pearly cheek*
> *The presence of Death avow.*

Pure little bud in kindness given,
In mercy taken to bloom in heaven.

Lincoln's son Tad, the youngest of the Lincoln children, was born with a severe speech impediment, a cleft palate, and deformed teeth. He was teased in school, as the children referred to him as "stuttering Tad." But Tad was tough and spirited just like his father, despite his disabilities.

Tad had a special relationship with his father, who was the president. It might have been said that he was a favorite child. So, when the president was fatally shot in 1865, Tad responded to the news by running through the halls of the White House screaming at the top of his lungs, "They shot papa. They shot papa." He grieved heavily but appeared to remember the lessons of overcoming adversity taught to him by his famous father. He said:

> *Pa is dead. I can hardly believe that I shall never see*
> *him again. I must learn to take care of myself now.*
> *Yes, Pa is dead, and I am only Tad Lincoln now, little*
> *Tad, like other little boys. I am not a president's son*
> *now. I won't have many presents anymore. Well,*
> *I will try and be a good boy and will hope to go*
> *someday to Pa and brother Willie, in Heaven.*

He developed pneumonia at the age of 17 and died just a few months after his 18th birthday.

Only one of the Lincoln children, Robert, would grow to adulthood. He was a strong and wise leader, seeming to follow in his father's footsteps. He was an honored guest at the unveiling of the Lincoln Memorial in Washington, D.C.

Abraham Lincoln overcame great political adversity in his life. He credited all he had personally suffered as the elements that prepared him for his most significant move: pursuing politics.

He developed a taste for politics in 1834 when he ran for the Illinois state legislature. He won handily due to his harsh stance on the horrors of slavery. He called for an end to the practice and promised to devote his life to its abolition. It seemed he had the golden touch in politics, winning two terms in the U. S. House of Representatives.

When the Kansas-Nebraska act was passed in 1854, allowing states to make their own decision about continuing slavery, Lincoln went back into politics in a run for the Senate, declaring that the country "cannot endure permanently half slave and half free." But he lost to the strong Democrat Party's opposition to ending slavery. Four years later, he decided to make a run for the highest office: the presidency of the United States of America. The Democrat machine rose against him with fierceness, but Lincoln fought hard and won the presidency.

Abraham Lincoln's leadership and ultimate abolition of slavery will live forever in American history. His was a life that seemed to end with the greatest adversity: death. But even death cannot stop a great man or woman. Lincoln was shot in a theater while he watched a play, presumably in retaliation for his work to abolish slavery. In assassinating him, though, his enemies immortalized him and glorified his legend. His international fame grew and the ideals for which he fought became entrenched in the American psyche.

Yet, behind the public accomplishments was a man who was deeply wounded from all the adversity he had suffered. He suffered from crushing depression his entire life. Friends reported that he spoke of his battle with depression publicly and often. Lincoln would often share with his friends that he saw the world as "hard and grim," and that he reportedly often felt worthless and flirted with the idea that suicide would be a welcome relief to his suffering. He told the man who was the partner in his law firm, "I am now the most miserable man living . . . Whether I shall ever be better I cannot tell; I forebode I shall not."

It is difficult for us, sitting on this side of history, to imagine a giant like Abraham Lincoln as a weak and broken man who struggled to survive the rigors of the day. He accomplished, arguably, more than any other president in American history. Each year various polling organizations like Gallup, Quinnipiac, and Gallup survey Americans, asking, "Who was the greatest president of all time?" Abraham Lincoln, the man who saw himself as a worthless man, ranks #1 year after year, almost exclusively.

We only have two choices in the face of adversity: step up or bow out. Though we wish we could change this, adversity offers us only those two lanes. It would be great if we could stand still and do nothing, but that is not the case. Even the choice to do nothing is a choice to give up and bow out. There is a powerful lesson in overcoming adversity in

Abraham Lincoln's life and legend. It is that your greatness cannot be measured from inside your own life. Life is not meant to be lived from the outside in, but from the inside out. We pour out on the world all that we have and all that we are, trusting in a miracle: that someone like us can make a difference.

This is a tall order, because when we look at ourselves from the inside, we see all of our faults and flaws. We see the areas where we do not measure up and think that, because of the dented places in our suit of armor, we are not qualified to make a positive and powerful impact on the world. But every person who has accomplished anything of value will join in the chorus of voices shouting in unison that it is *because* of your adversities that you are qualified to do what you are meant to do. Your adversities can teach you, propel you, open doors for you, encourage you, and strengthen you. Or, as in the case of Abraham Lincoln and perhaps in your own life, your adversities may humble you. They may bring you to the crossroads again and again and demand that you make a decision: step up or bow out.

Tragically, many people choose the latter. They give up on themselves, on others, and on life itself. They choose to be defined by their limitations rather than empowered by them. Why? They have their focus on the wrong thing. *They are focused on who they think they are rather than who they are called to be.*

Bowing out can take many forms. For some, it is falling into a state of helpless inaction. People who bow out in this manner think that by their inaction, they are escaping the difficulty of pushing themselves into a place that is difficult or unfamiliar. Indeed, that may be a scary place to move into. However, staying the same, unchallenged and unchanged, is a far more terrifying prospect.

Journalist and playwright, Fulton Ousler, brilliantly wrote, "Many of us crucify ourselves between two thieves—regret for the past and fear of the future." People who live in the tension of these two emotions are in a tragic state of suspended animation. They have tortured souls that can be easily freed by simply acknowledging a truth all humans must acknowledge: *I am not the person I am going to be.*

It is a powerful proclamation to makeover your life because it allows you to accept your current state without being bound by it. It also reaches for the future "you" and asks him or her to draw you closer to the place where the difficult, challenging, and unfamiliar becomes easy, commonplace, and ordinary.

It is possible to live from your potential rather than from your reality. We all do it, on some level, each day. Every time we take on anything new, regardless of what it is, we are living from potential. How do I know? When you tackle something new, what you are saying is, *I don't know what will be asked of me, but I believe that I will rise to meet the challenge.* It is what we do every time we apply for a job that is significantly different from the one we currently hold. For example, if you are a rank-and-file member of a corporate team and a position as the manager opens, it requires you to make a bold claim that you can do something you have not ever done before. You are living from your potential.

Another example is when you enter into a new relationship. You have met someone you barely know but sense a deep attraction to that person. You have no way of knowing all of the issues you will face as you navigate the new relationship. But you believe (and hope) that you will be able to build a long-term — perhaps lifelong — connection. You are living from your potential.

This kind of living trains you to deal with more sophisticated issues. It trains you to cultivate the best that is within you and present it to the world. You are saying to the world, "I think I have something to offer. I'm not sure, but take a risk on me. Believe in me." If you ask others to believe in your potential, you must also believe in yourself. You cannot ask others to do what you are not willing to do.

It is okay to be unsure. It is okay to fail. It is okay to take a chance that ultimately does not work out. What we must not do is fail to ever take the chance. Taking the chance is transacting on the future. And it usually pays off big dividends. Although you may never have 100% confidence, you can be confident in this: your past, no matter how difficult or troubled, was driving you to some future place. The only way you will get there is by letting adversity be the footing for your foundation and keeping your eyes fixed on the future. Our adversity provides us with the fortitude to succeed.

This is why we embrace adversity. You never know, at the time when you are going through it what adversity is preparing you for. It may be a trauma you suffered at one time whose usefulness is not revealed until years later. Never shun or abhor your adversities; instead, welcome them, because they are setting you up for future success by training your soul to be who you are called to be.

ADVERSITY LEADS TO ASCENSION

*There are moments when I wish I could roll back the clock
and take all the sadness away, but I have the feeling that if
I did, the joy would be gone as well.*

— **Nicholas Sparks,** *A Walk to Remember*

If you were alive in the 70s and 80s, you will recognize the haunting music that has come to characterize the movie *Jaws*. It was an instant success and became a cult classic. Famed director Steven Spielberg was the mastermind behind this movie as well as gems such as *Jurassic Park, Schindler's List, E. T.,* and *Raiders of the Lost Ark.* His name is synonymous with quality cinema. But as a child, the mind of young Steven was a place filled with fear and dread. He was bullied as a child because of his small size and pimply-faced appearance. The other students nicknamed him "Retard." He tells the story of a footrace between himself and another student and hearing the entire class cheering for the other guy.

Spielberg suffered from a host of adversities, including crippling night terrors and a fear of flying. He often refers to himself as having suffered PTSD from the adversities of his childhood. Even the tree outside his bedroom left him feeling afraid. Its imposing silhouette appeared to him to transform into a horrific monster whose snarling jowls and sharp claws threatened to crash through his bedroom window and devour him whole. He felt tortured by his imposing imagination. He said:

> *Every single night, my imagination would find something else to fear. I've always opted for waking up after a bad dream and being so happy I was awake, and then wanting to go back to sleep only to have drama again. There was just something about bigness that scared me when I was a kid.*

Spielberg idolized Lincoln and was mesmerized by the Lincoln Memorial statue. He said that standing next to the monument felt like standing next to a giant. Just like Lincoln, Spielberg had to overcome his past, confront his demons, and be empowered by adversity. His terrifying dreams and active imagination morphed into some of the greatest cinema the world has ever known. Spielberg has won 34 Oscars and been nominated for four times as many. He is a success story. But he had to overcome great adversity to arrive there. He used adversity as the catalyst for his long and fruitful career.

You must use adversity as a springboard rather than an obstacle. You will have to climb over the obstacle to use it to lift you to the next level. But that is the beauty of life: a seed is planted in the ground and covered by dirt as if it were dead. But being pushed down into the dirt is precisely what makes that seed grow. It springs up and begins to reach for the light. As it does, it produces a plant that is big and strong. That plant produces fruit and more seeds so that life can continue.

Adversity may be trying to bury you. If so, it's OK. You will not die. In the darkness, you will grow and develop. Soon, you will see the light.

Vera Wang was a quitter — at first. Before her 700-million-dollar fashion success, young Vera tried to have a career as an Olympic figure skater. She trained day and night, but she just did not have what it took to make it onto the team. So, she quit. She was sad and unclear about her future when she discovered a latent love for fashion. She did not become an Olympic skater, but her experience as a skater sparked her affection for the beautiful designs she and the other ice dancers wore. She was at a crossroads and decided to step up rather than bow out. She graduated from college and spent seventeen years working at Vogue Magazine. She became so smart and so skilled in her knowledge of fashion that she applied for the position of editor-in-chief. She suffered a devastating blow when she was rejected for the position. There seemed to be nowhere else to go. The only position remaining at Vogue Magazine to which she could be promoted was editor-in-chief. She had hit the glass ceiling and was facing another ten to twenty years before the position would open up again.

Vera was at the junction where she had to make a critical decision: let the adversity bury her, or use it as a medium to grow. She stepped up in a big way. Realizing that her career was at a dead-end and she was already 40 years old, she quit her job at Vogue and started at a new company, Ralph Lauren. But she soon realized this was not the right decision, either. Rather than get mired in fear, dread, and regret, she decided to start her own company.

Today, a baseline Vera Wang wedding dress starts at $3,000, but the most expensive one comes in at $1.5 million. Her fashion line is world-renowned. She said,

No matter how bad things get,
no matter how discouraged I feel,
no matter how much of a failure I feel lik
I try to believe there's a reason, there's a process,
and there's a learning experience.

Vera learned valuable lessons from her failures and ended up with a life that was far better than the one she would have had if any of her previous careers had been successful. Even her supposed failure as a figure skater became the building block for her unique couture. She continued,

> *All those years of skating and dancing have carried over. I can't design anything without thinking of how a woman's body will look and move when she's wearing it.*

ADVERSITY CONQUERS FEAR

We can easily forgive a child who is afraid of the dark;
the real tragedy of life is when men are afraid of the light.

— Plato

When you hear success stories like mine and others, it is easy to feel inspired and motivated. I hope you do. But I would also caution you against the ugly underside of adversity. What often causes us to bow out is fear. When we are staring down the barrel of adversity and there is an option that will alleviate our suffering temporarily, it is hard not to choose it. We are designed to avoid anything that may cause us pain or harm.

Life can challenge us with adversities that look like giants, monsters, or fire-breathing dragons. Cancer, divorce, bankruptcy, and job loss are all capable of forcing us to ask: Do I give up and surrender my life, my joy, and my sense of well-being in the world, or do I fight to be the kind of person who can face the challenge head-on?

Many people do choose to give up. Suicide rates around the world are disturbing. The U.S. ranks 27th in total number of suicides (up from 34th just 3 years ago) with nearly 50,000 people choosing to check out of life. That's pretty high for a country that is considered to be the land of opportunity, where dreams come true, and hope is just around every corner. For many who don't resort to such extreme measures, drugs, and alcohol help them cope with their inability to manage life. The opioid crisis in the U.S. has been in the news for several years, and with increasing frequency. More than 100 people die each day from opioid overdoses.

Thankfully, half of the world's population has never tasted alcohol. But for those who have, consumption — or overconsumption — is a real danger. According to the World Health Organization, people living in Ireland consume the most alcohol, at more than 14 liters per capita. Russians drink less than the Irish but have more alcohol-related deaths. Americans are more likely to be involved in a drunk driving accident than people in any other country.

Why are humans turning to these extreme measures to cope with their pain? Among the many reasons is fear. People generally fear the tough times: life's challenges.

According to many psychologists, there are some major fears we face as humans that cause us to run from adversity:

Fear of Our Inadequacy or Malevolence

We have spent sufficient time exploring the reasons why the fear of your inadequacy is misplaced. The fact that you are unable to complete a task or take on a challenge is more because you have not focused on your potential. But it is not just our inadequacy we fear. We also fear our malevolence. Soldiers often struggle with the acts that they have had to commit on the battlefield. They wrestle not only with the morality of the acts they have been ordered to perform, but they also grapple with their ability to kill or injure. In everyday life, we also fear our malevolence when we face hard times. Do we make a business deal that is right for us but harms someone else? Do we remain in a relationship knowing that our partner wants more from the relationship than we are willing to commit to? Do we retaliate against someone who has hurt us? These are the situations that cause us fear.

Fear of Society

There is a reason we grow up in families and communities. We need the safety that is provided by a close-knit group. The world can be harsh and unforgiving. Society has established all kinds of unwritten rules and judges us mercilessly if we do not stick to them. We are constantly trying to preserve our reputations, whether consciously or unconsciously. People have expectations of us. When we make choices that are right for us but not to their liking, they are quick to express their disappointment. If we try something new and innovative, they may even ridicule us.

Fear of the Unknown

Perhaps the greatest fear is the fear of the unknown. It has been said to be the fear that rules all fear. We like to have control of our lives, our money, and our careers. We even (ridiculously) seek to have control over other people. Even though we can never truly control another person, some people still try. R. Nicholas Carleton writes in *Journal of Anxiety Disorders*,

> *One fear to rule them all, one fear to find them, one fear to bring them all and in the black box bind them. The pastiche of Tolkien's text represents… the proposition that "fear of the unknown may be a, or possibly the fundamental fear" underlying anxiety and therein neuroticism.*

The way to overcome your fear is to keep your eyes on the prize. Like a runner, you must set your gaze on the finish line rather than the obstacles ahead or the competition running beside you.

Some have suggested that Abraham Lincoln was such an effective politician because he suffered great hardships and lived with depression. Without adversity, he would not have been able to lead the country the way he did. He would have been ruled, many suspect, by arrogance, egotism, and conceit. In many ways, his fight to end slavery was a personification of his enslavement. He was a prisoner of his mind and, as such, he understood the value of freedom in every form: physical, mental, emotional, and social.

ADVERSITY CREATES A NEW PATH

If the road is easy, you're likely going the wrong way.

— Terry Goodkind

The truth is that if we don't have to change, we usually won't. We are perfectly happy to keep doing what we have always done. When I found the light, it opened up a new lane for me. I *had* to follow that new path. If I remained where I was, I would continue receiving what I had been receiving in my life. I knew that I could never return to the dark place again. I had been given the opportunity for rebirth. But my new life would not be easy to create. I had to fight to reach for the light to be whole again.

One elementary school teacher shared the story of a science lesson she was doing with her young class of kindergarteners. The children, all aged 5, were given a butterfly enclosure to study and enjoy. They helped the teacher build the structure and set it up in their classroom. The only thing that was missing were the caterpillars. A week after the enclosure arrived, a special package housing their six new caterpillars came in the mail. The children were fascinated as the teacher carefully removed the caterpillars and placed them in the enclosure. The students eagerly learned what the butterfly larvae needed to eat and how their habitat needed to be set up so that they could survive.

Of course, the real show had yet to begin. The caterpillars soon crawled up on a branch that had been carefully secured inside the enclosure and began the magical process of spinning their chrysalises. Then the waiting began. The children watched day after day as the process unfolded. Their teacher calmed any anxious fears the students had by telling them each day that all six caterpillars were safe inside their chrysalises and that this process was necessary for the caterpillar to transform into a butterfly. The students seemed to buy that.

Imagine the joy the children experienced as the caterpillars began breaking through their chrysalises and sticking out little body parts trying to break free. The students gathered around the enclosure while the teacher sat at her desk, busily working. She glanced up from time to time to see what the students were doing. They were laughing and pointing at the enclosure and having a great time.

After several minutes, though, the children were still surrounding the enclosure. The teacher thought that it was odd that the children had spent so much time watching their caterpillars. By the time she walked over to where the students were gathered, she realized that there was a serious problem. The children had reached into the enclosure to help the creatures. They were very carefully pulling the chrysalises apart to free the caterpillars. They had ripped through five of the six cocoons before the teacher was able to stop them. The result was devastating. The five caterpillars who were "helped" out of their shells lay paralyzed on the bottom of the enclosure. They tried to flap their wings but could not. By the end of the day, they had died.

The last caterpillar, that the children had not had a chance to "help," finished the process of pushing itself out of the chrysalis. When it was done, it emerged as a spectacular butterfly and delighted the children as it flew around the enclosure. They released it into the warm, summer air to be free.

In a discussion later that day, the teacher asked the children why the five caterpillars they had "helped" had died, while the one they did not help flourished and soared. The children argued over whether one of the children had hurt the caterpillars accidentally when they were trying to help. The teacher lifted her hand to silence the children. She smiled,

> *You have learned an important lesson today. It doesn't matter whether you hurt the caterpillar when you broke open its chrysalis. The point is that you were trying to keep it from struggling to be free. What you did not know was that the struggle to break out of the chrysalis is exactly what the caterpillar needs. The struggle forces fluids into their wings and makes them strong. Without that struggle, their wings are never strong enough to take to the sky.*

It is a remarkable thing to watch the transformation of a caterpillar to a butterfly. It is consuming and exhausting for the insect. It must shed its old bug body if it wants to have wings that are strong enough and efficient enough to soar when the process ends. While it may be somewhat disgusting for us to imagine, it eats most of the rest of its shed body for nourishment. That means that it needs to get rid of what it once was to become what it wants to be. Even after it emerges from the chrysalis, it is not exactly ready to fly. It must hold on to the shell or risk falling to its death. The new butterfly still has a bit of changing and growing to do. Its wings are crumpled and wet and good for nothing. They must dry first; then the butterfly must practice stretching its wings before letting go of its old home and taking to the air.

We can learn a lot from the transformation of a caterpillar to a butterfly. The same sort of transformation was also true for me. I was at a point where I needed to change and grow.

It was a horrifying place, one that I could have allowed to take over my life and destroy my future. I wanted to take the easy way out. But everything I went through was part of the process I needed to go through to become the man I am today and to experience that life I have now. If I had had immediate success, I might not have learned the lessons I needed to learn.

When we think about our difficulties, it is critical to recognize that adversity forces us away from where we are and toward the place we are heading. We cannot go on as the same person we were. Adversity grinds the excess away from us and leaves us changed. What remains is far better.

You cannot carry into your future the weight of your past. Like the butterfly, you may need to completely remake yourself. Inside the chrysalis, the caterpillar is no longer a caterpillar. But it is not quite a butterfly, either. It is a strange in-between stage that scientists call a pupa. That is how it may be for you today. You are not quite what you want to be, but you are not what you used to be. Granted, it is an uncomfortable stage in life when you have shed your past but have not yet realized your future. Imagine the caterpillar upside down on a branch having to rebuild itself into something completely new. We call it metamorphosis — it is a super change, a complete restructuring.

Another lesson we can learn from the butterfly is that during the ten days of its transformation, it must survive without food, other than the dissolved body parts it eats to create its new form. In our world, the concept may look a little different, but the essence is the same. You will experience adversity in your life; that adversity is helping to shape and form you into the person you are becoming. In the meantime, though, you may have to live without some things. You may have to release some habits and attitudes that have been a part of you for your entire life.

Sadly, you may also need to release some people who have been scaffolding in your life. You know about scaffolding. It is the temporary structure erected around a building, used only during the construction phase of the building. It is not pretty, but it is necessary to the process. But once the building is complete, the scaffolding is removed so that the beauty, and more importantly, the functionality of the building can be seen and utilized. The same is true for you when you are suffering from adversity. The people who bring "drama" into your life serve you just as well as the people who bring you joy. The "drama ushers" can teach you to have more patience, kindness, endurance, and forgiveness. They can teach you how to hold your tongue and keep the peace. They can teach you how to love unconditionally. But they are not meant to be a part of the overall and permanent structure of your life. They have come only for a season. And just like the passing of seasons, they move on when their season in your life ends.

Have no misgivings about acknowledging that a season with a particular person or activity has ended. That is the power of adversity. It comes in waves and teaches you to navigate through storms and circumvent obstacles so you can become a master at navigating and circumventing! It shows you where you are in life so that you can make your next big move.

It would be a mistake to carry too much from your past into your future. Some elements of your life may have a purpose for where you are today, but they may not accommodate where you are going. Be brutally honest with yourself about what those things are and where changes need to occur. As Maya Angelou said,

You may encounter many defeats,
but you must not be defeated.
It may be necessary to encounter the defeats,
so you can know who you are,
what you can rise from,
and how you can still come out of it.

When adversity comes, it is often because you are moving to a new place. You are heading in a new direction. You are figuring out how to forge a new path. When you write the next chapter of your life, you will use the difficulties you have endured as your springboard to take you to the next place. Your approach may have to change based on the circumstances you face.

The COVID-19 Pandemic of 2020 is a perfect example of the power of adversity to force us from where we are onto a new path. From an educational perspective, the pandemic forced the closure of schools in 192 countries, meaning that more than 90% of the world's students had a new way to learn. Many schools decided to suspend classes for the rest of the 2019-2020 school year. The long-term effect of this decision is impossible to calculate at this point. Only history will be able to successfully determine what students have suffered or gained. But experts have estimated that the loss of a third of the school year may impact their future economic opportunities.

Parents who wanted to save the 2020-2021 school year had to make some major shifts and adjustments. They could no longer rely on the school. It was up to each mother and father to supplement their children's education so that they could succeed in the future. It forced parents onto a new path. Some parents handled it as a challenge. They worked hard to find opportunities for their children. Other parents complained and gave up.

The challenges of the pandemic created a wider variety of learning opportunities for many students. Parents, teachers and students discovered more about what style of learning worked best for individual children. Many students had new learning options. This was one blessing of the adversity many faced due to Covid-19.

A pandemic is the kind of adversity whose tendrils reach every sector of life. But the same is true for almost all major sources of adversity. When adversity strikes, it is like a battering ram. It pushes us from where we are into a new place. And almost instantly, we have to learn how to steer in that new lane.

You may be moving into a new lane in your life. How exciting! Perhaps you would say, "This is not exciting; this is terrifying." It is both. It is scary because you are entering new territory — uncharted territory. It came upon you suddenly. You have no time to prepare. You have no emergency action plan in place. You barely have any money set aside. You have no new skills to get you through the crisis. You're lost in a wilderness. It's terrifying. To that fear, I encourage you with the words of Eleanor Roosevelt:

DO IT AFRAID!

You are in a place where only courage (not money, schooling, or resources) can carry you through. There are plenty of people who had money in reserve but were not able to make the transition when their industries vanished. They needed other skills to survive.

Perhaps the greatest skill I needed to develop was courage. Courage stands up to adversity as nothing else can. Courage is not the absence of fear. Courage is the ability to remain vigilant when fear is staring you in the face and threatening to destroy you.

One great example of a courageous person is Jackie Robinson. Long before Rosa Parks sparked a national protest with her defiant refusal to move to the back of a segregated Montgomery, Alabama bus, Jackie Robinson had already taken the same stand on a bus in Fort Hood, Texas. He was court-martialed for taking his stand. But he believed that he had served his country in World War II and deserved his seat on the bus since he had put his life on the line for his country. He fought his court-martial relentlessly and ultimately won.

Robinson's foray into major league baseball had little to do with his desire to play. It was about fulfilling the mission of his life: to create a world where opportunities are equal everywhere. He even broke the ranks of MVP by earning a spot in the All-star game and playing so well that he was named the National League's Most Valuable Player. As Sam Haber said in *My Hero Sports Stories,*

> *Robinson worked all his life to make it to the big leagues and fight for civil rights. . . Robinson's actions toward desegregation went beyond the game of baseball as well. He was active in civil rights organizations and worked with various politicians in both parties.*

> *In 1964, he became a civil-rights adviser to Republican Governor Nelson Rockefeller of New York. . . Even after he finished fighting for equality in baseball, he continued to work towards national equality at the political and secular levels afterward. . . Jackie Robinson was a brave and strong-willed ambassador for integration who worked throughout his life to benefit not only himself but the lives of others.*

Robert Downley Jr. is another example of a person having the courage to find a new path. After years of alcohol and drug abuse, and stints in rehab and many relapses, Downey made a life-changing decision to find the light. He had wallowed in the darkness for a long time. He had seen a light and began chasing that light. His pursuit of the light began his road to recovery. He chose to steer into the skid because he knew that he was meant to work as an actor, but he needed to take a new approach. He embraced rehab and added it to his new skills of meditation, prayer, yoga, and therapy.

On his new path and with the help of some friends, the string of hit movies began to roll out and continues to this day with films like *Zodiac*, *Kiss-Kiss-Bang-Bang*, and *Tropic Thunder*, for which he received an Oscar nomination. Even bigger hits were in store for Downey, including *Chaplin*, *Sherlock Holmes*, and a string of movies as the character Iron Man in the blockbusting *Avengers* franchise.

One example of a company that found a new path because of adversity was the Lego company. The company started because its founder, Ole Kirk Christiansen, was looking to use the excess lumber from his business. His furniture creations were an instant hit, but a string of tragedies (including a fire and the stock market crash) forced him to choose a new path. He decided to change from making ironing boards and chairs to wooden toys. At first, it seemed that he had made a mistake, changing from a furniture shop to a toy shop. But Christiansen had fallen in love with making toys.

His toys started catching on, particularly a set of interlocking blocks that could be used to build different toys. Once again, adversity struck. Fire consumed his factory and he lost all of his materials and inventory. Christiansen was in a dark place for the second time in his life. He decided to make the switch from wood to plastic. The company enjoyed massive success and then tragedy struck again with the death of his son and another fire that destroyed all of the wood on-site. The new leaders decided to abandon the flammable substance of wood in favor of plastic. The modern lego toy was born and the company has been the most profitable toy company in the world with a net worth of more than $14.6 billion.

Adversity provided multiple course corrections to create a product that millions of children enjoy and use creativity every day. Imagine a world without legos!

We do not always know how to create a new path. We are not designed to see around corners. It is much like a person on a long road trip at night. The headlights only illuminate a few feet ahead. As the car moves forward, the next few feet become visible. A person can travel across the country by just being able to see a few feet at a time. And you can make it to your destiny even if you can only see the next step. You may not know what is waiting for you down the road. You don't have to. Just keep moving. As the biblical text promises in Isaiah, chapter 43:

> *Remember not the former things,*
> *Neither considers the things of old.*
> *Look, I will do a new thing;*
> *Now it will spring forth;*
> *Will you not know it?*
> *I will even make a way in the wilderness,*
> *and rivers in the desert.*

Paths in the wilderness and rivers in the desert. That is what miracles are made of. They are those special gifts that come to us at just the right time, in the most unexpected places and unexpected ways. They are the new paths that adversity offers us.

ADVERSITY CLARIFIES VISION

Darkness cannot drive out darkness: only light can do that.
Hate cannot drive out hate: only love can do that.

— Martin Luther King Jr.

We can all think back to seasons in our lives when adversity seemed to come again and again in waves, like rivers of difficulty. But adversity has always had a definite purpose: to clarify your vision. If you are reading this book, it is probably because you have experienced adversity in your life and want to learn how to move past it. Perhaps the title caught your attention because you have experienced the darkness, desperate for any hint of light. Or perhaps you know that present and future adversities are working in you (and out of you) something useful for a greater or higher purpose.

One of the ways we manage the emotions and uncertainty around difficult times is by framing them in the context of the larger vision and purpose of our lives. If you are going to embrace the light and step out of the darkness, you will need to alter both your conversation and your mindset. You must know, believe, and understand that there is a great treasure inside of you. Often, that treasure is hidden because it is buried beneath the mountain of adversity you may have faced or may be facing right now. To unearth your unique treasure, you must shift your conversation from negative and limiting self-talk and adopt a new vocabulary.

No longer can you speak about your tough times from the "woe is me" perspective. Rather, you can choose to speak about your adversity for what it is: tools that help you to see life in a brand new and positive way. As you change your conversation, you will inevitably change your mind. Often the conversation change precedes the mindset change. That is ok. As you talk through these paradigm shifts, you come to understand that they serve you rather than victimize or control you. You will find that, over time, your mind begins to accept that nothing that happens to you is wasted. It all goes into the rich stew that is your experience and helps to make you more and more effective in everything you set your hand to do.

The image of following your North Star can give you powerful imagery that transforms your conversation and mindset. This approach believes that every person has a North Star. It is the light that we can see in the distance, like a beacon leading to our purpose.

This North Star is like an inspiration, a guiding light, that illuminates the path forward. This is true for all people, no matter what their purpose turns out to be. They may be people who save lives or people who serve coffee. It does not matter if the mission appears to be menial, because there is no such thing as menial when you are moving toward your destiny. You are accomplishing the purpose you were placed on earth to do. Menial does not mean meaningless. We learn that what we do should not be judged by how big an impact it has, how many people it reaches, how much money is earned by it, or the opinions of others about it. It can only be measured against what each of us feels called and appointed to do. The best measure of a victorious life is if you are doing what you were meant to do.

What often happens with a small vision is that it can grow far beyond anything you imagined it could be. A seemingly insignificant act can grow to be a life-changing calling. There is no way to know in advance if a venture is going to be successful. The important thing is to just get moving. Just like the Magi in the time of Christ, you must follow your star. At the end of their journey, they discovered the greatest gift humanity had ever experienced. So overwhelmed were they with their destiny, that they heaped gifts of great value upon the Christ child.

Historians and theologians have calculated that, upon finding Christ in a lowly stable, they gave him gold, frankincense, and myrrh that would today be worth a great deal of money. The magi realized that all of their worldly possessions had no significance anymore because they had found something that had greater meaning.

That is what happens when your vision is clear, and you know that what is in front of you is the thing you were always meant to see. The wise men would never have experienced this if they had not followed the star. If your star is moving, you should be moving too.

Henry Ford had not done much with his life, but he was good at repairing and rebuilding watches, and he had vision. His father had given him a pocket watch as a gift, which Ford took apart and put it back together. He was so fascinated with its inner workings that he began to offer to rebuild watches for people in the community

Ford spent long days and nights on his father's farm. Any spare time he had was used to rebuild watches. He left home at sixteen to pursue a job as a machinist and later a bookkeeper. You can see the building blocks being formed for the ultimate purpose of his life. As he was working these various jobs, he was nursing the vision of a horseless carriage. He knew that it would need a power source and felt sure that it could be powered with gasoline.

He built his first buggy in 1892. In 1913, Ford had the idea to create an assembly line similar to the ones he had seen in meatpacking plants. People thought this idea was insane. Cars had always been built in one spot. The thought of moving a car along a line, adding parts to it along the way, seemed absurd. But Ford started assembly line production and was able to produce a working vehicle in just under 3 hours.

This would prove to change the entire country and hundreds of other industries, because the cost of production dropped from $850 to $310. It meant that average, working middle-class people could own a car. The invention of the assembly line Ford Model T gave workers job stability, caused the collapse of the railroad industry, and opened the door to new engine design.

But it was not all roses for Henry Ford. He lost investors' money and upset them with his revolutionary ideas and many years of trial and error and failure. Ford adopted the philosophy that:

**FAILURE IS SIMPLY THE OPPORTUNITY
TO BEGIN AGAIN, THIS TIME MORE INTELLIGENTLY.**

This helped him make it through the failure of the Model A and the 5 years it took to produce the successful Model T. His vision was refined by adversity and in the end he created a whole industry and the company that bears his name is strong and successful over 100 years later.

What is your vision? Where do you see yourself in one year? Five years? Twenty years? Or, more importantly, what do you want to have said about yourself at the end of your life? Will you have done the things you set out to do (at least in your heart)? Will you have righted the wrongs that plagued you? Will you have left behind a legacy that will be remembered by at least one person?

There are important questions. But far too many people do not ask these questions, and even those who do often fail to answer them. You have to be clear about your vision and write it down. Something very powerful happens when you write out your vision. First, it is one way to deepen your commitment to your purpose. It is also a way of helping you to plan out the steps that will help you achieve your goal.

That is what I did during those long months of incarceration. I began to think and explore all of the gifts I had been given and the interests I had. Rather than worry about where I was 24 hours a day, I spent a lot of time planning where I was going with my life.

If you do not have a vision, do not fret. This is a wonderful and exciting opportunity in your life. You are unlimited. You have a blank slate upon which to write the biggest, boldest, wildest dreams, knowing that it does not matter whether or not you have the resources, knowledge, or any other elements to bring it to fruition. You only need the courage to commit.

Your goals are powerful because they help you to identify the distance between yourself and your goal. Don't spend time worrying right now about whether or not you have the money. You cannot wave a magic wand and make your goals suddenly appear. All you can do at this point is begin the process. While the specifics may be different for each person, the journey is the same. It starts with making a decision, summoning the courage to commit, and beginning the process of taking the very first step.

There is little difference between a person who needs a thousand dollars and a person who needs a million. They both are going to have to figure out what they have to do to overcome their obstacles. They must embark on a quest to find the money. Once the man needing a thousand dollar taps the well, his need will be met. The same will be true for the man needing a million dollars. Being hung up on what you do not have is simply a mental stall tactic. Resist the urge to even think about it. Just get serious and then get busy.

In the famous film, *The Secret*, Rev. Michael Bernard Beckwith makes a bold claim. He writes:

You can start with nothing,
and out of nothing and out of no way,
a way will be made.

ADVERSITY REBUILDS FOUNDATION

*Throughout the centuries there were men who took first steps
down new roads armed with nothing but their vision. Their
goals differed, but they all had this in common: that the step
was first, the road new, the vision unborrowed, But they won.*

— **Ayn Rand,** *The Fountainhead*

Adversity is like fire. If you have seen the after effects of
a large building fire, you will have noticed that the wood has
turned to ash. All of the roofing material is melted. Walls

that once stood erect have disappeared. But the steel that held up the building usually remains intact. The concrete foundation is untouched and undamaged. Based on that solid foundation and the steel construction, the building can be shored up and rebuilt to exceed its former glory.

Could it be that the same thing is happening to you amid adversity? Your troubles probably feel like scorching fire right now. And as a result of what you are going through, you are losing a lot. But consider for a moment the possibility that whatever you are losing was not intended to be a part of you forever. Just like the butterfly or the scaffolding, the image of the fire is meant to teach us that some of the things we have collected and attached to our lives are not intended to be permanent. So the fire comes along to remove the excess and make room for what is sure, strong, and long-lasting.

You must build yourself a strong foundation. I realized when I went into jail that my foundation was quicksand. It was my poor foundation that had me involved with the wrong crowd. When the fire came, it burned up everything weak in my life. When I looked around, I could see that I had nothing solid or sure to stand on. It was time for a new foundation. This time, I would build one that would stand strong and endure many trials. I built one that could be tested by fire and emerge strong and solid.

Building your foundation begins with your vision. No matter what comes, that foundation must be unshakeable. As you tear away the past, you will be building something new. You may not know exactly how you are going to do it. You must reject any insistence that the "how" is available to you at the start. It will not be. But, as you begin to move into the next phase, clarifying your vision, you will find that the how begins to unfold — slowly at first. Just like a well that is being tapped for the very first time, you will only have trickles of water. But over time, it will pump an endless supply of life-giving water.

That is why we write the vision. That is not metaphorical: you must take that literally. Sitting down with a piece of paper and a pen to write your vision is a bold and effective step. Even from a secular standpoint, writing your vision has been proven to be one of the most important ways to achieve great things in the world. A University of Scranton student and followed a group of people for one year, from the time they set their goals at the start of the year (New Year's Resolution) through to December 31st of the same year, to determine how many of them had achieved their goals. The student found that 92% of people made little or no progress, and all of the 92% had abandoned their goals long before the year was even half over. The 8% who did achieve their goals were the people who took the time to write their visions down.

After you write the vision, you must take time to clarify it. Make it plain. Define it step by step as far as you can. You might only be able to identify the first few steps and the final step. That's OK. Over time, your purpose will unfold and become clearer and clearer. Making the vision plan involves clarifying the vision and making it so obvious that only a decision to neglect or ignore it could stop it from coming to fruition. As an anonymous person said:

Your vision will become clear
when you look into your heart.
The person who is outside can only dream.
The person who looks inside will awaken.

You are off to a great start. You have defined your vision and put it on paper. The next step is to get busy listing your goals. This step will have many nuances. Let's try to cover them all. For starters, you must be prepared to act on your vision. No matter what the vision is revealed to be, unless you are willing to run with it, there is no point in writing it and no point in clarifying it with a master plan. As Joel A. Barker said,

Vision without action is merely a dream.
Action without vision just passes the time.
Vision with action can change the world.

Your vision must be so powerful, so strong, so insightful that it makes you want to get up and run. Many people use vision boards to help them get moving on their visions. They take a large poster board and fill it with words and images that help to keep their vision front and center. This is both a practical and a spiritual experience. From a practical perspective, this helps you stay focused. But from a spiritual perspective, seeing your vision helps you to grow your faith. As your faith expands, your ability to seize the things you want in life also expands. You find that you are moving closer and closer to your vision. At the same time, your vision is moving closer and closer to you. One day, you will achieve synergy when you hold your goal in your hand. As the saying goes,

**MAKE YOUR VISION SO CLEAR
THAT YOUR FEARS BECOME IRRELEVANT.**

Seeing your vision also helps to quiet your fears. You will always have fears and worries and concerns. But when the vision is in front of you, the fears are less pronounced. There will always be setbacks. You may take a small step forward only to find that you have to take two steps back. That is also a part of the process. In every step, whether forward or backward, you are gaining valuable knowledge that you can use for the next leg of the journey. Thank your lucky stars that you are smart enough, strong enough, and brave enough to face setbacks with the courage of a thousand soldiers.

I have seen it all in my journey. I have come face to face with the good, the bad, and the ugly. I have had many challenges in my life that I worked to overcome. The greatest struggle, by far, was the struggle against false imprisonment. It is one thing to have your freedom taken away because of something you did. But when you are completely innocent and lose your freedom, it creates a hole in the heart that is deep and wide.

Some people have never been behind bars, but they live in the prison of the mind. They are constantly stopped and undone by their fears. Others are stopped by their anger. Others are stopped by the friends in their circle who continually bring them down when they are trying to get a leg up in life.

I don't know what a "perfect" life is. I was taught to never envy another person or covet the life they are leading. It is impossible to tell by looking at someone what kind of life they are living or have lived. As the poet said, "Into each life, some rain must fall." No matter how idyllic a person's life looks from the outside, they have paid a hefty price to be where they are today. No one escapes tough times. It does not matter how much you have going for you; it cannot shield you from adversity. We all experience death, loss, sickness, and pain of some kind.

You can see the power of thought in my life. Thoughts truly do become things. Someone once said that luck is when opportunity meets preparedness. I set about preparing myself mentally so that I could later prepare myself financially when I got out of jail. I was determined that as soon as I was released, I would jump in with both feet. I had experienced success before, but I knew that my prior success was just the tip of the iceberg. I could do more now because I knew more.

Looking at my life from the outside, it may seem that I have everything. But looking from the inside, you will see the adversity, the pain, the struggle, the hurt that has accumulated over many years of fighting to be me in a world of people who found my very existence to be an affront to them. Everything that glitters isn't gold. Even the most valuable diamonds are far from beautiful to look at when they are first mined. They are rough and dirty. They don't have smooth edges. Their surfaces are bumpy and hard-edged. Their color is cloudy and dim. But as the jeweler polishes the diamond, its brilliance starts to come into view.

The process of polishing sounds gentle — almost idyllic. You get the image of some sweet old jeweler gently refining the precious stone in a quaint village shop. But the reality of polishing is far from that sweet image. It takes a very rough surface to polish a diamond enough to release its splendor. It is almost like grinding. But when the process is complete, what emerges is something of great value and high demand in the world. The same is true of you and me. We may be rough around the edges, or cloudy in our thinking or our understanding of our purpose on earth. It takes the rough rub of adversity to polish us and clean us up and present us as valuable in the world.

I am blessed in that, although I have witnessed firsthand the worst evils that reside in the human heart, I have also seen the very best humanity has to offer. I have experienced the power of the human heart to turn from hatred to love and to find ways to connect with people whose story differs from their own. For that, I am most grateful.

Reflecting over my life, even the times that were dark and dreary, brings me joy. There is so much to remember — some good days, and some days I wished I could end it all. I reached out to help everyone I could. Now, I can't stop giving myself to the world — I'm so much of an extrovert, I could make a friend in an empty room. I love to talk to people and find out who they are, to connect with them and get to know them. Reflecting on life like this helps us to adjust and fortify our foundation.

But none of my life experiences have been free of adversity. That is the great challenge of adversity. When things are going well, it is easy to find reasons to show gratitude. But, when hard times come, we think that all is lost, and we have nothing to be thankful for. That is why I encourage people to stop in the middle of their adversity, take a breath, and focus on what matters to them. Taking your eyes off your troubles and putting them on what is important will go a long way toward helping you receive the light. When you do, you will find that you are flooded with blessings. The gift of breath is just one of the many bounties you enjoy. For many, during the global pandemic, we had the time to reflect. But we spent so much time worrying about all that was happening around us, we were missing the gifts that were right before our eyes.

It is interesting what you can do when you are alone and can gather your thoughts. You have time to plan and strategize. You can determine the outcome of your life's journey. There is a saying that is full of life and wisdom:

Put 100 random people in a room, hand them five sheets of paper and ask them to write down their five greatest problems. Then have them fold each of their five sheets of paper and place them in a pile on a table in the center of the room. Then invite them to reach into the pile and pull out any new five problems that will magically become their new problems. Once

everyone has taken their five new problems, give
them the choice of taking their new problems or going
home with the ones they came in with. Odds are,
people would choose their original problems.

I believe that this is true. I would not want anyone else's problems. I have had my share of laughter and tears. But I would not trade them. The bumps along the way have shaped me. Adversity is tough, but it has its benefits. Even though it comes in wave after wave of misery and sadness, you learn how to handle it. And just when you think you cannot take another hit, along comes another hit. So, you stand even when you cannot fight because you know that in standing, you live to fight another day.

Everyone has a story to tell. My life is different from the lives of others. But some similarities thread through every person's life. We all have joy and pain. We all have adversities that we must overcome. We all have times of sickness and times of health. And while we may not all make a difference, we certainly all have the opportunity to change the world even if it is only in some small way. That is what I have done with my life. I have worked to change my corner of the world.

There are many kinds of adversity I have faced. Perhaps you have, too. When you give of yourself and pour out of your heart, and your time, and your energy to help others, it often sets up an expectation in their minds that you are obligated to do so forever. So, when you don't meet that expectation, the response is not, "Thank you for all you have done in the past." Instead, it is, "How dare you; you should do more."

I refuse to surrender to the pain of this mindset. Life is all about choices. The choices we make determine the outcomes we will experience. I choose to live. I choose to love. I choose to forgive. This is my foundation.

There was a time when humans had to function as one. It was the earliest of days on the earth. We were so few that we had to stand as one people if we wanted to survive. We were not concerned with the differences that separated us. After all, everything in the environment was set to kill us. Imagine it! There were more animals than humans. We needed to work together to outlive and outlast the creatures that wanted us for food. With no long history to guide us, we have to learn how to live on this rock. We had to discover where to find food, how to build shelters, and how to cure ourselves when we were injured or sick. We had to contend with the ravages of heat or cold. There were more reasons to work together than fight with each other.

However, as we learned the lessons of survival, and humans became more abundant, we also learned the lessons of separation, evil, and hatred. We taught ourselves to make distinctions between ourselves and others based on meaningless criteria, like the color of one's eyes, the amount of money someone has, or the shade of their skin. We put barriers between ourselves and trained our hearts to hate because of those barriers.

We allowed these meaningless differences to eat away at the fabric that had kept us woven together as people. It is as toxic for those who perpetrate it as it is for the victims of it because, at its root, it is fueled by hatred. Hatred is blinding to the eyes, the mind, the soul, and the spirit. Like a man with no eyes, those who fail to spend their lives on purpose and foundation stumble around in the darkness of their rage and evil. Shining the light on these people who have dwelt in the caves is equally blinding. Their eyes, having seen and known only darkness, fail to adjust to the light. So, they turn away, cover their faces, and wince in pain. They refuse to look into the light.

It takes great courage to look into the light. It can be painful. The light will expose what is good about us and what needs a major overhaul. The light does not discriminate. It shows us our strengths as well as our weaknesses. We live in a society where we look for perfection from others. We judge people by the tattoos they have on their bodies or the clothes they are wearing. We make assumptions about people's worth based on body size, or eye color, or pedigree. Who is this picture of perfection people are trying to find? Does this person exist on planet earth? It is easy for us to forget that life itself is the thing that is precious. Just the fact that the person is breathing is enough for them to have value. They should not have to replicate an image of perfection that has been arbitrarily determined by others, who, incidentally, also do not fit the picture.

Even Hitler, who demanded that everyone reflect the picture of the Aryan race (tall, blond with blue eyes and broad shoulders), did not meet that measurement himself. He had dark hair and brown eyes. He was not tall, and he had dumpy shoulders. Still, he murdered, gassed, and burned six million people for not meeting his standard. The same is true of the colonizers who raped and pillaged African peoples and enslaved them. They portrayed them as weak and dull-witted. Yet these are the same people who built their homes, planted their crops, raised their children, and worked their entire lives with little rest to build the nation we call America. That is the insanity and psychosis of the darkness in the human heart. It has no basis in logic or reality. It is the work of madness to those who embrace it.

Life's journey is not a straight road, as the poet, Robert Frost, wrote in his poem, *The Road Not Taken*. He emphasizes the powerful effect of choosing the road less traveled: "*And that has made all the difference.*" I believe that I have traveled that very road. Even though I am an extrovert with a very gracious and outgoing personality, I traveled a very unique road. It is amazing how the road of life works sometimes. The road we travel is long and winding. Sometimes it is a smooth and easy path, lined with willow trees and flowers. At other times, there are lions, and tigers, and bears. There are ditches and chasms to cross. There are boulders to climb over. That is why a solid foundation for your life is so important to build. You never know what is just around the bend, waiting for you. That has been my road in a figurative sense.

I made a promise to myself, to my boys, and to the world that I would give the very best I had within me. I made that promise because I felt I had an obligation to give whatever portion of light I could to anyone who needed it. The great thing about the light is that you can give it away and still have plenty for yourself. The more light you shine on others, the more you have to give. It is a resource that never runs out. It is amazing how making others happy can improve your self-esteem.

I had to learn to fight the urge to let the pain and suffering I was experiencing inform my decisions. I had to develop an inner motivation and self-confidence. Self-confident people don't go around making others miserable, the way some of the men in jail did. They had so much anger and rage in their heart, they used it to harm those around them. This made jail life the most hostile and verbally abusive environment a person could encounter. And their rage was not something I could physically escape. I was there day and night. I saw. I heard. I felt. It was always there. But I could mentally and spiritually escape, if I was willing to put in the work that was required. Many of the men just gave up. You could see the light go out in their eyes. You could hear their hearts break in two. I do not blame them for doing so; jail life is nearly unbearable. But that was not a decision I could make. I chose to face it and fight it every day of my life. If I had given up the fight even one day, perhaps it would have consumed me too.

I love libraries. I find them to be life-giving in their ability to shift your mind from a consumer of news, opinions, and entertainment, to a mindset that is centered and focused on the power of knowledge. I am struck by the grandeur of a library. The sights and the smells immediately tell you that you are in a unique place, and there is no other place like it on earth. There is no shortage of knowledge in this world. It is all contained in the pages of the books we refuse to read. When I opened my mind, knowledge came flooding in and it changed me profoundly.

Life is filled with reasons to rage, cry, fight, and embrace anger. There is enough tragedy and pain for each of us. And you can be sure that we will all get our fair share. But adversity comes to teach us the lessons of forgiveness. We learned, in our misery, to find the miracles. And when we fix our eyes on them, we see all that is beautiful in God's amazing world.

Reinventing yourself is the order of the day. People must perform the magic trick of turning on a dime and immediately shifting their focus from something they knew to something they've never known and were wholly unprepared to tackle. Perhaps you are reading this book during your own hard time. But as difficult as things may seem right now, there is always a flicker of hope. We often hear the term "new normal" and wonder what people mean by that. What they mean is that now is not the time to mourn or lament what was lost. Now is the time to look forward to the next chapter of your amazing life. To that end, I will make a bold claim: It doesn't matter one bit how old or young you are, how rich or poor you are, how educated or uneducated you are, or how connected or unconnected you are when it comes to reinventing yourself. That is the power of reinventing. It means you can start over. As Oprah Winfrey says,

Your future is so bright, it's blinding.

REINVENTING YOUR LIFE

*It's never too late or, in my case, too early to be whoever
you want to be. . . I hope you live a life you're proud of.
If you find that you're not, I hope you have the
courage to start all over again.*

— The Curious Case of Benjamin Button

We talk about second chances and beginning again with idealistic romanticism. It looks so easy in the movies and reads so well in books. It is the perfect third-act resolution. The guy gets the girl. The business is magically saved. The hero wins. But the reality is rarely ever so glamorous.

Starting over is one of the most difficult tasks a person can take on. Let's face it: starting over is usually necessary because the way we started in the first place crashed and burned, necessitating the task of starting over. Something we poured our hearts and souls into did not work or was taken away from us in some unceremonious fashion. Now we are left with the ashes and the broken pieces of a marriage, career, business, or a life in general.

Though you may be walking in a cold and barren wilderness, you must not succumb to fear. Something great is in store for you. It may be new. It may be frightening. It may cause you to dig deeper than you ever had. But what you will discover will be nothing short of miraculous. You may discover the diamonds in the depths.

Your life is not over when you have been swept up by adversity. It is just beginning. The same wind that brings the damaging storm also brings the refreshing rains that replenish areas stricken with drought. The same fire that sweeps through the forest and leaves it looking bleak and barren, forces new acorns to explode and release their seeds into the fertile ground. These new seeds, once planted, turn into vegetation nourished by the life-giving potash from the remains of the fire. The fire clears the underbrush and nourishes the soil.

Step back and reassess your situation as if you were an outsider looking in. From the inside, you have to manage the emotions that are in play. But from the outside, you can observe as a bystander and get started crafting a plan to put it all back together.

Your new life is not going to look like the old one did. That is a fact you must accept. But that is not necessarily all bad news. If we are honest, there are things about our old life that we would gladly surrender. Unfortunately, they were attached to a lot of the things we loved and treasured most in the world. That is what makes the separation from the life we had so painful.

Forget all the mistakes of the past, but do not forget the lessons you learned from them. Those lessons are the catalyst that will carry you through to the next level of greatness. Your yesterday is nothing compared to what your tomorrow is going to be.

I had to start over and rebuild my life almost from the ground up. Starting over means you can take on life better than you were before. You are older, smarter, and wiser than you were when you began your journey the first time. Just the experience of failure makes you more resilient and incredibly powerful.

You can seize the pain or seize the power. But you can't hold onto both at the same time. If you elect to embrace the new power, you have to wield your magic wand and make your life what you always wanted it to be in the first place. Granted, some dreams may be long gone. Perhaps you always wanted to be a ballerina. Now you're 52 years old and unable to pursue that dream. But could you be an instructor? Open a dance school? Work for a ballet company? There are a million possible iterations that your dream could take. You just need to start exploring.

Don't give up. I have never failed because I have never quit. So long as there is breath in your body, you have opportunities. You might think it's easy for others to say, "Don't give up." They don't know what you've been through. They don't know your struggles, your debt, your loss, or your pain. Well, it is not easy for anyone to say. It is one of the hardest things to say: "I am not giving up." But once you convince yourself to say it (and repeat it a couple of times), it starts to unlock those parts of your brain that shut down when you are despondent and ready to quit.

When you begin to speak positively about your life and its circumstances, your brain lights up like a Christmas tree. It is alerted that there is a problem to solve and it sets about solving it. Neurons begin to fire and, all of a sudden, an idea pops into your head that seems to come out of nowhere. But it did not come out of nowhere. It came from your mind, which you activated when you decided to press through the pain and reach for the future.

People all over the world are hurting. Many are suffering from the worst loss of all, the loss of a loved one whom they couldn't be with to hold as they took their final breaths. For others, the loss has been a loss of security. Long lines at the food banks are a stark reminder that we are a country woefully unprepared for any kind of crisis. Seventy percent of Americans have no money saved. The majority of people in the West admit to having no financial plan. They are in survival mode living paycheck to paycheck.

The same is true for many companies. Any kind of major tragedy hits companies hard because they are so intricate and complex and have a million moving parts. The task of rebounding from the effects of a downturn will be difficult. The key is to learn from the mistakes we have made and begin again with a new paradigm that is more suitable for long-term success, no matter what calamities strike us.

In adversity, your dreams get a second chance to rise and guide your future. But you will need to allow yourself enough time to set yourself up for success. You will need time to get the training, do the research, and explore the options. Perhaps you are thinking, *I'm out of time!* If you have a mortgage coming due, bills to pay, and no food in the refrigerator, time is not a luxury you can afford. There are some things you can do to speed the process. Warning: It will require you to be a bit uncomfortable and step outside of your comfort zone.

Give yourself time. One of my greatest lessons was to learn to give myself time. I did not have to do it all at once. This reinvention (or transformation) is not likely to happen overnight. It sometimes takes time for people to uncover who they are and what they want out of life. We spend so much time walking the path others have carved for us, that we forget our right to carve the path ourselves. As Benjamin Franklin said:

MANY PEOPLE DIE AT TWENTY-FIVE AND AREN'T BURIED UNTIL THEY ARE SEVENTY.

Starting a new life is like beginning a new day. Is it scary? Yes. But it brings with it some very wonderful and positive gifts. Starting over could be the most amazing thing that has ever happened to you. What an incredible thought.

If you are like most people, your previous life seems to have happened to you so fast, you were always playing catch up. Many of the things that occurred were beyond your control. Other things were well within your control, but your inability to stay ahead or your neglect caused you to look around one day and wonder, "How did I get here?" You often flirted with the idea of making some changes. But you were too entrenched in life, job, business, or marriage to get the ball rolling toward growth and development.

When adversity strikes, it brings a brief but golden opportunity to start again with the reins firmly in your own hands. You are no longer a victim of circumstance. You are now an active participant helping to craft and shape your future. Now you get to decide what path you will take. And while it may seem like there is no path forward, you know deep in your heart that the opposite is true. A path will become clear to you as you take the necessary steps to move forward. You may only know the first step. That's ok. Take that step and then wait. You will find that the next step becomes clearer from your new vantage point.

Always remember that a path will be made, even through the roughest waters, the mightiest wilderness, and the most desolate of deserts.

ACKNOWLEDGEMENTS

I would like to thank God for His grace and mercy on me. I would also like to thank my mentor Dick Harp for believing in me. To everyone at O'Leary Publishing including April O'Leary, Heather Desrocher, and Juliann Thomason for all the content help and to Jessica Angerstein for this beautiful book design. Big shout out to Louis Venne for amazing photography. To my Jamaican community friends on Clubhouse thank you for your support including Angela Acosta, and many others. And last but not least to my sons Rajay, Kamryn, Karter, and Cornell Bunting Jr, my step-daughter Zoie Beazer and my fiancé Natuschka Beazer. Thank you for your love through thick and thin. We are truly blessed.

ABOUT THE AUTHOR

Author and motivational speaker, Cornell Bunting connects to his audiences through his words. The power of his writing inspires and entertains children and adults alike. His own harrowing story is one of survival, inspiration, and motivation. He is the author of 7 books. Bunting was born in Jamaica, raised in Bristol, England, and resides in Southwest Florida with his four sons. To find out more visit www.cornellbunting.com